JOHN DEMOS

PURITAN GIRL, MOHAWK GIRL

AMULET BOOKS ~ NEW YORK

Cataloging-in-Publication Data has been applied for and may be obtained from the Library of Congress.

ISBN 978-1-4197-2604-0

Text copyright © 2017 John Demos
Illustrations copyright © 2017 Greg Ruth
Book design by Pamela Notarantonio and Melissa J. Barrett

The artwork on the facing page and used throughout the book is based on a wampum from the collection of the Library of Congress. *Wampum: To-ta-da-ho belt*—diamonds in center said to be a covenant chain signifying alliance of towns. Call Number: LC-B2- 29-15 [P&P].

Printed and bound in U.S.A.
10 9 8 7 6 5 4 3 2 1

Amulet Books are available at special discounts when purchased in quantity for premiums and promotions as well as fundraising or educational use. Special editions can also be created to specification. For details, contact specialsales@abramsbooks.com or the address below.

ABRAMS The Art of Books
195 Broadway, New York, NY 10007
abramsbooks.com

For Violet and Clover,

this book's first readers,

with love

from their papou

CONTENTS

When Christopher Columbus and other explorers got to America from Europe, they found millions of people already living there. They didn't know where they had landed, or who those people were. They thought perhaps they had reached the Indies, a group of islands in Asia; that's why they called the natives Indians.

After a few years, as more and more Europeans came over, they realized that America had nothing to do with Asia, and that these Indians were a completely different group. They saw America as a "new world." They settled on the land and claimed it for themselves. They started farms, villages, and towns. They organized "colonies" that belonged to their home countries in Europe. They didn't ask permission from the Indians; they just went ahead with their plans. They viewed Indians as inferior to themselves—as "savages" living in a primitive way.

In fact, the Indians and Europeans each claimed certain advantages over the other. Europeans took pride in their sturdy wood houses, their skills in making cloth and ironware, and, most of all, their Christian religious faith. Indians were better at growing crops, at moving about in the wilderness, and at hunting and fishing; moreover, they were confident in their own religious practices. Both sides were eager for trade. For example, Indians would offer the fur pelts of beavers and other animals caught in the forests, while Europeans gave woven blankets, iron pots and knives, and glass beads in return.

The earliest European colonies were founded around the year 1500 in Central and South America and the islands of the Caribbean Sea, by people who came from Spain and Portugal. Then, in the 1600s, English men and women began coming to places along the Atlantic coast of North America that are now within the United States. At about the same time, the French founded a colony in what is Canada today.

The various European countries involved in this colonizing were often at war with each other. And whenever that happened, their colonies were dragged in, too. Some of the bloodiest wars were between the English in New England (the colonies of Massachusetts, Connecticut, New Hampshire, and Maine) and the French in eastern Canada. They were rivals for the land, as well as in religion. The French were Catholics; the English were Protestants. The Catholic Church had been the only one in Europe for many centuries. But in the early 1500s, some of its members split off and started their own church; they became the Protestants. Each side thought of itself as the only true religion; each condemned and hated—and sometimes fought with—the other. This was true in the colonies of America just as it was in Europe.

As time went on, native peoples were pulled into these struggles. Though their populations were going down throughout the 1600s and 1700s—mostly because so many died of diseases brought over by the colonists—Indians were still a force to be reckoned with. Their biggest, most powerful grouping in eastern North America was the Five Nations of the Iroquois. Each of the five lived separately, but cooperated with the others in trade and warfare. (In 1722, one more nation was added, and the Five became Six.) Their territory covered much of what today is upper New York State. Most of this group were friendly toward the English colonists and bitterly hostile to the French. There were, however, several small clusters, chiefly Mohawks (one of the original five nations) who had left their homeland and moved northward into Canada. There, they became allies and trading partners of the French. Some lived in what were called missions, villages founded by French priests with the aim of persuading as many of them as possible to become Catholics.

In the early 1700s, England and France began a war that would go on for about ten years. Almost immediately the fighting spread to their American colonies—New England against French Canada. Some of the Iroquois sided with the English and others chose to stay neutral, while the Mohawks in Canada actively joined the French. There were bloody raids back and forth. Whole villages were destroyed, and hundreds of people were killed. The "French Mohawks" (as they were now called) captured many colonists, especially in New England, and took them to Canada. Some would be returned in exchange for ransom, but others were held for years—decades even—and adopted into native families. Quite a few would never go back to their homes; in many ways, they *became* Indians.

This book is about one of the captives, the most famous of all: a child with the English name of Eunice Williams. If somehow we could visit New England in the 1700s, we'd hear about her from the people living there. Almost everyone knew her story.

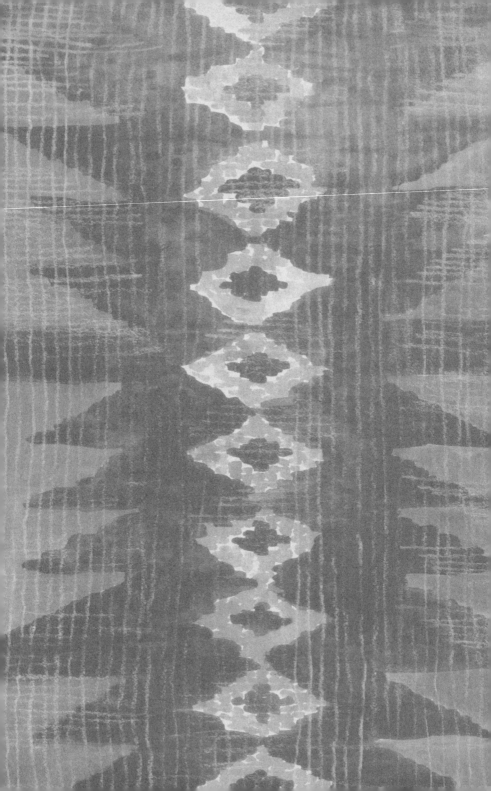

PART ONE
PURITAN GIRL

CHAPTER ONE
WINTERTIME

"LISTEN!" EUNICE SAID, SITTING UP STRAIGHT. "Don't you hear that rustling sound out by the summer garden?" It was midnight. Beside her in the little wooden bed, her older brother Stephen lay snuggled beneath a heavy quilt. She nudged his shoulder, and he woke up. "Listen," she said again, lowering her voice to a whisper. He nodded and cocked his head to one side. Together they strained to hear. She was seven, he was ten. The rest of their family was fast asleep.

Eunice climbed out of bed and tiptoed to the window. Outside the moon shone brightly, making the trees cast long shadows across the snow. As the wind blew, the shadows moved from side to side; one was shaped like a crouching person. Eunice's eyes moved with it, sensing danger. But when she looked some more, everything seemed normal. She was about to turn away when she heard it again—the same sound, but clearer now, more like a crunch than a rustle. At the window, she again peered out. Then she saw, off to the left, a tall figure walking slowly back and forth, his boots breaking the crust on the snow. A musket was tilted over his shoulder. He was the night watchman, standing guard. Feeling relieved, she climbed back into bed.

Her people—in the town called Deerfield, which was part of the English colony of Massachusetts—were at war with the French up in Canada. It was the winter of 1704; enemy soldiers might be coming any day. Her father, Reverend John Williams, had warned her, and told her to stay close to home. "Mark my words, child," he said, "no one is safe. We must pray to our Lord for protection every day." Her father was a minister and town leader; whatever he said must be obeyed.

Some of the Indians were enemies, too. They knew the forest better than anyone; they could blend into the trees and move without sound. You couldn't tell they were there till it was too late. They liked to attack in the dark, when the townspeople were sleeping. That's why Deerfield needed a night watchman.

The next morning dawned bright and cold. Eunice and her older brothers trudged through the snow to the small red house where Granny Hinsdale ran the village school. Inside, all the children sat in rows on wooden benches. They were of different ages, ranging between about six and fourteen. The teacher divided them into groups and made different lessons for each one. Eunice and the other littlest children were learning the alphabet. Each had what was called a hornbook, a small, flat piece of wood with a piece of paper pinned to it that was covered with see-through strips of cow's horn; on the paper, all the letters were written. The children would read and recite the letters aloud from A to Z, sounding like a chorus. The older children were practicing numbers—adding, subtracting, counting to a hundred. At the end of the morning, they all stopped what they were doing and listened as the teacher read them stories from the Bible. She read the same story three times, then told the children to recite it back to her in the same words. Eunice had a good memory and could do this quite easily. "You are a smart child," the teacher said to her. "It's God's gift to you; use it well."

After they got home, Eunice and Stephen put on their warmest clothes and went out in the yard to play. Together, they piled up snow to make a fort. They broke off tree branches to use as pretend muskets. They got their brothers, Samuel (who was thirteen) and Warham (who was four), to act like enemies coming at them through the woods. Eunice and Stephen hid in the fort, then sprang up with a shout, pointing their branch muskets. Warham fell on the snow, pretending to be dead, but then got up and danced around. Stephen said a little crossly, "Stop your fooling; this is serious! The French and Indians might really be coming. We've got to be ready."

Throughout that month it snowed and snowed. Most days after school, the Williams children played for a while and then went about their chores. The older boys would go to the barn to feed the animals and clean their stalls, while Eunice stayed in the house to help with women's work.

On some afternoons Eunice chopped vegetables for a stew her mother was making for supper. When she was finished, she would go to the hearth, stand on her tiptoes, and dump the whole lot into a big kettle that hung from a hook in the chimney. She had to be careful around the burning embers, though. Once when she went too close, her skirt caught fire. Luckily, Samuel was nearby and threw a pail of water on her to make it stop. She wasn't hurt, but the skirt was ruined.

Another of Eunice's chores was pushing the handle on a wooden churn that turned cow's milk into butter. Up and down it went till her arms ached and her fingers grew stiff. Sometimes she closed her eyes and tried to distract herself by humming tunes she had learned from one of her cousins in Boston.

When she had time, she also sewed. She was making what people called a sampler. This was a square piece of cloth on which she stitched colored threads to form letters and numbers, along with flowers on the edges. When at last it was done, she sewed at the bottom: *Eunice Williams of Deerfield Her Sampler Finished 11 of January 1704 in the 8th Year of Her Life.*

That was the pattern on weekdays, but Sunday was completely different. They called it the Sabbath, which meant it was all about God. No one did regular work. Instead, they spent hours in church, first in the morning, then again in the late afternoon. Whole families went there together. The grown-ups sat in long pews, with the men on one side and the women on the other. The children were up in the balcony with a man called a warden making them behave. If they talked or giggled, he lifted his cane and rapped them on the knuckles. Eunice always sat beside her friends Martha French and Mercy Carter; in the wintertime, when it was cold in the church, the three girls snuggled together under a large blanket that covered all their legs and laps. Eunice's father stood down in front and led everyone in prayers. He also preached sermons that went on and on; sometimes it was hard to stay awake.

The church was for Protestants, like all the others in New

England. Some people called them Puritan because they tried to practice an especially "pure" kind of religion. The way Eunice understood it, you were supposed to think only good thoughts and to love God even more than your own family. In fact, she did better than most. She said her prayers every night, and always tried to treat other people with respect. People said she was a true Puritan girl.

CHAPTER TWO

A BABY SISTER

AS THE WINTER WENT ALONG, EUNICE'S mother was expecting a baby. Her stomach grew bigger and bigger. She didn't always feel well, and sometimes had to spend all day in bed. When that happened, a dark-skinned woman named Parthena who had lived with the family for several years took charge of the children. In some ways Parthena was a second mother to them; they loved her, and she loved them back. Every morning she would brush out Eunice's long blond hair and form it into a beautiful braid. Often she told fascinating stories about life in Africa, where she had been born and raised. She didn't mention being captured away from her own family, brought by ship to America, and sold as a slave. And Eunice never thought to ask her about it.

There was lots to do before the baby came. Parthena

went to the attic and got the cradle they used when the other children were born. Mice had gnawed a large hole in the bottom, so it had to be fixed. There were clothes to find and arrange, and bands of heavy cloth they would wrap around the baby's whole body—what they called swaddling—to keep it warm and safe.

Many of their neighbors helped with the preparations. Goody Nims brought a wool blanket she had made last summer after the sheep were sheared. ("Goody," short for "goodwife," was what married women were called, while "Goodman" was how you referred to a man.) Goody Allen and Goody Corse had both made pincushions with embroidered designs, a common gift when a baby was about to arrive. Goodman Barnard and Goodman Field brought firewood to use in cooking and for keeping warm. Eunice and her brothers piled it in a tall stack beside the barn.

But the most important person in all this was the village midwife, Goody Frary. She was an older woman no longer able to bear babies of her own but skilled in helping others have them. From time to time she would stop in to see how Eunice's mother was doing. The two of them had been friends for years; Goody Frary had delivered all the Williams children. This was a comfort since giving birth was risky; you couldn't be sure of how it would go. Every evening the family sat together at their dinner table and prayed for the safety of both baby and mother. Eunice tried not to worry, but she couldn't help thinking how terrible it would be if something went wrong and either the baby or her mother died.

Finally, on an afternoon near the end of January, Mrs. Williams felt the start of labor pains; the baby was coming! Reverend Williams went off in a hurry to get the midwife, who lived at the other end of the village. Snow was falling as he rolled the carriage out of the barn and harnessed two horses to pull it. Soon the flakes became so thick he could hardly see. But he made it through and found Goody Frary eating her supper. As soon as he appeared, she knew the reason. She grabbed her overcoat and rushed to the carriage; there was no time to lose.

While this was happening, Eunice went out to call several of the neighbors. When someone gave birth, it was the custom for other women to help the midwife. Eunice ran from house to house telling them: "The baby is coming! My mother's pains are getting stronger! Please come quickly!" Within minutes Goody Allen, Goody Nims, Goody Hawks, Goody Sheldon, Goody Corse, and Goody Munn were all there at the Williamses' door. At almost the same moment the carriage pulled up, bringing Eunice's father and the midwife.

Now they all went to the "borning room" at the back of the house. This was a little room used only for giving birth.

Parthena and the neighbor women spread blankets on a bed in the middle. They brought towels to use when the baby was coming out. And they filled pails of water for washing up when it was over. Goody Frary had a little bag of ointments and medicines that she arranged, one by one, on a bench in the corner. Mrs. Williams walked slowly into the room and sat on the edge of the bed. Her pains were increasing, but it wasn't time quite yet. The others hugged her and promised to do their best.

Then they made a circle around the bed, held hands, and lowered their heads. Reverend Williams came in from the parlor to lead them in prayer. "Almighty God," he said in a trembling voice, "have mercy on all your servants gathered in this room, and especially on my dear wife and the child whose life is about to begin. We pray that they be preserved in good health, to join the faithful here on earth for years to come. But if, instead, they must go now to sit beside you in heaven, we will say with all our hearts 'the Lord's will be done.'"

After he finished, Reverend Williams went back to the parlor, where he and the rest of the family would wait. The children were very excited and tried not to worry too much. Eunice and Stephen played games of pick-up sticks and marbles to distract themselves. Every so often they would lean toward the door, eager to hear some hopeful sound—maybe even a baby's cry.

Meanwhile, inside the borning room, Mrs. Williams lay back on the bed and closed her eyes. The other women stood on either side of her, rubbing her neck and shoulders and humming soft tunes. Then, when the baby was close to being born, they called to her: "Push! Push! Push!" And so she did. Moments later the midwife said, "Look, here comes the baby right now!" She held it gently in the palms of her hands and lifted it up for all to see: a tiny, beautiful girl.

The other women dropped to their knees and gave thanks to God. The baby made a little cry, just loud enough for the family in the parlor to hear. Reverend Williams opened the door and led the children in. He said a blessing, then gently kissed the baby on top of her head. Eunice gave her a big smile and touched the tip of her tiny nose. "Now I have a baby sister!" she said proudly. "I love her so much!" The whole family rejoiced.

For the next few days both mother and baby stayed in the borning room. Parthena went in often to make sure they were doing well. The baby slept a lot, and only cried a little. Eunice tried to be as helpful as she could; sometimes she straightened the swaddling bands or gently washed the baby's face.

When a week had passed, Reverend Williams said it was time to baptize the baby in church. Everyone went except Eunice's mother, who was still regaining her strength after giving birth. The baby was in a christening gown, a beautifully embroidered silk dress made for the occasion. Inside the church it was even colder than usual; Eunice, though wearing her heavy wool cape, was shivering as she watched. There were special prayers and hymns. Then her father dipped his hand into a big basin of water, sprinkled several drops on the baby's forehead, and said, "I baptize you, dear Jerusha, and commit you to God's care." That was the name he gave her: Jerusha. It came from the Bible. (Eunice had been named after her mother.)

After another week Eunice's mother was strong enough to go back to her normal life. But first she gave a small party for Goody Frary and the others who had helped with the birth. Parthena set out pies and cider in the parlor. No men were there, only women; it was a way for them to celebrate what they had all done together. Eunice came in carrying the baby, who was dressed in the same lovely gown. "Jerusha, Jerusha," everyone called out, "how sweet you are! And what a pretty name you have!"

CHAPTER THREE
ENEMY ATTACK

THOUGH ALL WAS WELL INSIDE THE
Williams household, out in the village the worries grew
stronger. The war with the French and their Indian allies was
going badly; other towns nearby had already been attacked.
Scary rumors flew around. Some people had seen footprints
in the woods nearby. Others had heard strange sounds from
across the meadows. Then there was a night when the moon
shone red, like blood.

Sixteen soldiers came to Deerfield and moved into the
town stockade, a special fortified house built of heavy logs,
to protect the townspeople. Carpenters repaired the fence
that surrounded the village center. Some families living on
the outskirts decided to come in close and stay with relatives
or friends. On Sundays, in church, Reverend Williams led

prayers for everyone's safety. When Eunice and her brothers went off to the schoolhouse every morning, Parthena walked with them just in case enemies appeared. But as one February day followed another and there was no actual sign of the enemy, people began to think that maybe the danger had passed.

The last night of the month—February 29, because it was a leap year—started as usual, with supper, then prayers and bedtime. Soon all the houses were dark, and the families asleep. The night watchman patrolled the roadways and saw nothing unusual. Eventually, as the night deepened, he sat down to rest. Everything was quiet, except for the soft sound of a lullaby coming from a house where a mother was trying to soothe her wakeful child. After listening for a few minutes, the watchman dozed off. The lullaby ended, and the village lay still. The moon was a thin sliver rising in the east. Sunrise was still several hours away.

At that very moment, enemy scouts were hiding in a field just to the north. When they saw the watchman asleep, they signaled to the large group behind them— fifty Frenchmen in full military uniform and two hundred Mohawk warriors in thick wool cloaks and war paint. They had trudged through deep wilderness for weeks from Canada, waiting for just this chance.

Silently, with their hatchets and muskets held ready, they crossed the field. They climbed the snowdrifts piled against the fence, crawled over, and dropped down on the other side; from there they scattered to different parts of the village. Just then the watchman suddenly woke up, realized what was happening, and let out a shriek: "To arms! To arms! Enemies in the street! Everyone prepare!" But it was too late; the attack had already begun.

At the Williamses' house, Indian warriors were bashing their hatchets against the front door. They finally kicked it open and stormed inside. Eunice, fast asleep just a moment before, leaped from her bed in the front room and raced to the kitchen. Her brothers ran here and there—to the attic, to the cellar. Her father barely had time to grab his musket and aim it at the Indians. He squeezed the trigger, but it didn't fire—which was lucky, since, if it had, they would have killed him on the spot, and the rest of the family, too.

Eunice crawled under a table and buried her face in her hands. Minutes passed; shouts and screams filled the air, but in the darkness she couldn't tell from whom. Then, when a French soldier came in with a light, she crept back into the front room and peered around. She saw her father bound with a rope to a chair a few feet away, with spatters of blood on his nightshirt. She saw her mother kneeling beside the feather bed, her eyes closed, softly praying. She saw her brothers, who had been brought from their hiding places and shoved into a corner. She saw Parthena—sweet, kind Parthena—sprawled across the floor. And she saw, finally, the tiny form of Jerusha, her baby sister, cradled in Parthena's arms. Both just lay there, not moving at all. Eunice could tell that both were dead, but why? Had Parthena refused to hand over the baby?

Eunice was so shocked that at first she just felt numb. She told herself it must be a nightmare from which she would soon awake. She closed her eyes as tightly as possible. But when she opened them again, she knew it was all real. Her throat felt choked; she could hardly breathe. When one of the Indian warriors came and lifted her off the floor, she wailed with terror.

As the attack went on, one house after another was taken. Only at the stockade was there much of a fight. The soldiers there held out for almost two hours, aiming their muskets through the upstairs windows. It was a furious battle. Twice the Mohawks rushed forward with burning sticks to set the building on fire, but were driven back. But when they tried a third time, it worked. With flames rising around them, the soldiers had to come out and surrender. They, along with many of the villagers, were captives.

The Mohawks took the whole group to the church and made them stand against a wall. There were more than a hundred of them, mostly families with children. Eunice and Warham were among the youngest. They clung to each other, sobbing loudly. Some of the Mohawks tried to comfort them. Their father had told them that Indians were kind to children, and soon they would find out if it was true.

The French soldiers had left to attack another town, so the Mohawks were in charge. Their plan was to take most of the captives back to Canada, a journey of over two hundred miles. It would be very difficult, especially in winter. The Mohawks looked everybody over to see who would be strong enough to survive. There were several old people and two very pregnant women whom they decided not to take; these were set free. The rest would have to go on as best they could.

CHAPTER FOUR

THE JOURNEY

THEY SET OUT THAT SAME AFTERNOON. The Mohawks insisted on going as fast as possible, in case English soldiers were trying to catch up from behind. The captives were told to walk in a line, almost like it was a march. Mohawks were at the front and rear, and along the sides, to prevent anyone from escaping.

The Williamses were right in the middle. Eunice and her mother walked together, holding hands. Warham was too small to keep up and had to be carried by his father. The older boys, Samuel and Stephen, were just ahead. Sometimes they all sang songs, to boost their spirits. Occasionally, Reverend Williams tried to encourage others in the line. "God watches over us and will keep us safe," he'd call out. The woods were thick, and the snow was deep; with every footstep, they sank in.

When the sun set, it was time to stop for the night. The Mohawks prepared a camp in the woods. Supper was what they called *kanontara*—a mush made from dried corn and beans, mixed with snow and heated over a fire. Eunice didn't like the taste, but she was hungry so she ate it anyway. Afterward the Mohawks brought blankets and animal skins to keep everybody warm. They took all the men to a separate area and tied their hands and feet to tree trunks; that way they couldn't run off in the dark. The women and children huddled beneath a clump of fir trees. Eunice and Stephen lay down next to each other on a bit of ground that was clear of snow and covered with moss; at least it was soft. But it was so different from their bed and home, and they found it hard to sleep.

The next morning the Mohawks got everyone up before sunrise in order to make an early start. They walked all day, following a rough trail. They crossed a frozen river and climbed a small mountain. Even though Eunice and her brothers were strong, they found it very tiring. From the top of the mountain, they could look back and see Deerfield. Before leaving, the Mohawks had set fire to most of the town, so now there was only a pile of smoldering ruins. The captives knew that had happened, but still, they were shocked to see it. Eunice could just make out what was left of her own house. Everything familiar was gone.

In the afternoon, as they walked on, snow began to fall and the wind rose. The cold seemed to reach to their bones. Stephen stumbled on some rocks and hurt his leg, but still kept going. Another boy fell into an icy stream and had to be pulled out; the Mohawks wrapped him in blankets to stop his shivering. But Eunice's mother, still weak after giving birth a month before, had the hardest time of all. She would take a few steps and then have to rest, which made her lag behind. Finally, she stopped and sat under a tree. She told the others she couldn't go any farther. Eunice nestled beside her, anxiously looking up into her face.

Several of the Indians came running and talked excitedly among themselves. What should they do with her? She couldn't be carried like a child on such a long journey. But if they left her behind, she would freeze or starve to death, or be attacked by wild animals. It was best, they decided, to end her life right there.

They used hand signals to explain it to her and say they were sorry but could do nothing else. And Eunice's mother soon understood what they were signaling. She hugged her husband, her children, her Deerfield friends and neighbors, and said goodbye. As Eunice sobbed, her mother held her tight and whispered in her ear, "You must be strong, my sweet one, after I am gone; your dear father will always take care of you." Everyone was weeping. They formed a circle around

Eunice's mother, knelt in the snow, and prayed together for her soul. Then two Mohawk men took her away, out of sight; when they came back, she wasn't with them.

Eunice and her brothers huddled together, their bodies limp, their faces streaked with tears. Reverend Williams, too, struggled with his grief, but knew he must be strong for the children. He took them into his arms one by one. He told them their mother was in heaven now and would never again have to suffer.

The Mohawks stood to one side and allowed them time for this. Then, with darkness falling, they made another camp in the forest. Again the men were tied up to prevent escape. For the Williams family, it was the longest, saddest night they had ever known. Eunice cried herself to sleep.

The next day was like the previous ones: walking, walking, walking. With new snow underfoot, it was more difficult than ever. Eunice did her best, but finally it was too much. One of the Mohawks saw how tired she was and lifted her onto his back. She didn't know how to feel about this; it was confusing. He was among the men who had ruined her home and taken her mother's life. Yet he and some of the others seemed friendly. Anyway, she had no choice. From this point on, she, like Warham, was carried.

Others in the group were also having difficulty. Goody Brooks developed a bad cough and then a fever. Goodman

Kellogg lost his gloves, and his fingers froze. Eunice's father had large sores on his feet. Years later, in a book he wrote about being captured and walking to Canada, he recalled how every night he had to wring blood out of his socks.

The days turned to weeks, and still they went on. The weather warmed up and turned the snow to slush. They crossed more rivers and climbed more mountains, till they finally came to a great lake. You couldn't see across it to the other side, and there were islands in the middle. The French called it Lake Champlain after one of their leading explorers; the Indian name for it was Oniataroten (meaning "standing water"). The ice on the lake had melted, and there were canoes waiting along the shore; they could travel from here by water. There were enough canoes to hold everyone. Clearly, the Indians had planned their attack very well and made provisions for the long march back. The captive men had to help with the paddling, while the women and children rode as passengers.

By this point the captives had grown used to the wilderness, to the overnight camps, to the strange food, to sometimes being cold and wet. But lake travel was different, with its own risks and problems. Eunice was in the first canoe, crouched in the middle. She didn't know how to swim and was afraid of falling overboard. The canoe just behind hers was leaky and had to be abandoned. Another hit a rock and overturned;

a woman nearly drowned. Whenever the wind rose it made waves on the lake, and everyone got splashed. However, they did move faster on the lake than they had on land. And if the weather was clear, they could see for miles. There were tall mountains on the western horizon. Once, as they paddled near the shore, a mother bear and two cubs came ambling out of the forest. Eunice watched the cubs romp happily at the water's edge while the mother lay down to nap. Another time, she saw a moose wade right into the lake and splash around. High overhead, eagles and hawks swooped through the sky.

Eunice rode with the same man who had carried her through the forest. He was her captor and the one who looked after her. Sometimes he would speak to her in his own language while pointing here or there; with enough repetition, she could begin to grasp what he meant. He sounded out his name—*A-ra-kwen-te*—and she sounded out hers. She never stopped thinking of her mother, though; it was a constant sorrow. She counted on seeing her father and brothers, and most of the time they were nearby. She looked forward to nighttime, when they could all lie down and go to sleep together. That was when she felt the safest.

Before setting out one morning, the Indians decided to divide all the captives into smaller groups. This, they thought, would make the travel go faster. But it meant that the Williams family would be split up. When Eunice realized what the plan was, she ran to Arakwente. She flung herself on the ground, weeping bitterly. He picked her up and tried to calm her. But when she continued to cry, he carried her to his canoe and put her in it. Then he climbed in behind her and started off. Her father stood on the shore, helplessly waving goodbye. When she tried to wave back, her arm wouldn't move; it was like she was paralyzed, she was so sad.

From this point on, Eunice was in a group with Arakwente, six more Indian men, and two other children from Deerfield, Martha French and Joseph Kellogg. Both of them were her friends from before. It made Eunice feel a little better that they could talk together and comfort each other. After more days on the lake, the Indians decided to leave their canoes behind and again travel through the forest. As before, Eunice rode on Arakwente's back. They headed off on a wide path that would lead them straight northward, into Canada. From time to time they passed groups of Indians going in the opposite direction. Whenever that happened, they would stop to pay their respects; sometimes there were long speeches of greeting in Indian languages. Once a young warrior wearing a large feathered headdress smiled at Eunice and motioned toward her as if he wished to take her with him. She was very afraid and ran behind a tree to hide. But Arakwente shook his head and waved the other man off. He was her protector now.

They came to a large Indian encampment where they were invited to stay overnight in a tipi. The next morning, they joined their hosts in a hunt for game. One man killed a deer and brought it back to the camp, where the women built a fire big enough for roasting whole joints of meat. Then they had a feast and ate and ate until not a scrap was left.

A few days later, as they continued along the path, they met another group with several captives, including Eunice's brother Stephen. His head was shaved except for a ridge down the middle, and he was dressed in woolen blankets Indian-style; at first Eunice hardly recognized him. But of course they were happy to see each other. They hugged and sat side by side, talking about their recent experiences. And they prayed together, just as their father had taught them. Pretty soon, though, their masters said it was time to go. After they parted, Eunice felt more alone than ever.

CHAPTER FIVE

CANADA

BY NOW THEY WERE IN CANADA, NEAR
where Arakwente lived. It was a large village set alongside the
region's biggest river, the St. Lawrence, and home to many
Indians of the Mohawk nation. Its name was Kahnawàke
(meaning "besides the rapids"), and its people were called the
Kahnawakenerons.

The first thing Eunice saw as they approached was a tall
fence made of wooden posts that surrounded the village.
Arakwente gave a shout to announce their arrival. A large
wooden gate flew open and several Indian children came
running out. When they saw Eunice—still on Arakwente's
back—they gave her smiles of welcome. One little girl
reached up and stroked Eunice's hair, but Eunice was scared
and shrank away.

A minute later a very tall man emerged through the gate. He was dressed in a deerskin tunic and leggings and had dark tattoos all over his face. He and Arakwente embraced, laughing, and began a loud conversation. Eunice couldn't understand much, though by now she did know a little of their language. She thought she heard the words for "fire," "forest," "snow," and "white people." After a few minutes the tall man turned to her and bowed low, but again she shrank away. It was all so strange and frightening. She held back her tears, but felt a terrible longing for her own family.

Suddenly Arakwente strode ahead, carrying her right through the gate and into the village. Just inside was a big open area, like a public square. Arakwente put her down and pointed here and there. On all sides were houses that looked very different from the ones in Deerfield. They were long and thin, shaped like tubes lying flat on their sides. Their walls were made of branches set in the ground and bent over on top to form a roof. The outer covering was strips of tree bark.

In the middle of the square was a well where several women were filling pails of water. Beyond that stood a large building made entirely of stone, with a tall bell tower and wooden crosses in all the windows. Eunice thought it might be a church, yet it looked nothing like the one in Deerfield. Later she found out that it was a Catholic church. Her own people, the Puritans, didn't like Catholics at all. In fact, everything Eunice had heard about them was terrible.

As she stood there, more of the village children came running up and made a circle around her. They wore linen shirts and leggings with leather moccasins on their feet. Some had little strings of beads hanging from their ears. They stared at Eunice and giggled at her appearance. Her clothes were ragged after so many weeks of traveling in the wilderness; her wool cape was practically in shreds. She wished she could go off somewhere and hide.

Then Arakwente walked on, motioning her to follow. They went down a narrow path to one of the longhouses, apparently his own. A young woman—maybe Arakwente's daughter, Eunice thought—ran out to embrace him, but didn't seem to notice Eunice. They went inside, which was all one room. There were no windows; the only light came in through the door. It took a minute or two before Eunice got used to the dimness and could see well enough to make things out.

Along the sides were wooden platforms with straw mats and fur pelts scattered on top. The floor was dirt, and scuffed. There was a pit in the middle—a fireplace—with a hole overhead to let the smoke out. A large kettle hung over a bed of glowing coals, filled with what Eunice thought must be their dinner cooking. There were metal pots and barrels made of bark in one corner, and dried fruits and vegetables hanging from a beam overhead.

Eunice thought of her own home in Deerfield, so far away and now destroyed. She pictured the wide brick hearth and chimney, the glass-paned windows, the beds with feather quilts, the spinning wheels, the stores of grain in the pantry, the apples drying in the cellar. How different this Indian home seemed! How dark! How strange!

An older woman of perhaps Arakwente's age sat by the far wall. She was weaving thin strands of wood to make a basket. But she dropped her work and rose to her feet as the group came in. She and Arakwente stood facing each other, their hands joined but saying nothing, for several minutes. Then she looked toward Eunice and gave her a gentle smile. Arakwente pulled the two of them together and looked back and forth between them. He spoke directly to Eunice, saying the woman's name—Konwatieni. Eunice understood that she was his wife.

Just then a child came into the house. She was one of those who had giggled at Eunice's appearance, and Eunice realized that she must be part of Arakwente's family, too. She stared at Eunice, but this time it was in a friendly way. Eunice thought the girl seemed about her age. Suddenly the girl skipped off. When she came back, she was carrying what looked like a little doll without a face; it was made from a cornhusk. She held it out to Eunice, obviously intending it as a gift. But Eunice just stood there, dazed.

Soon more people entered the cabin: another woman, a much older man, two very young girls, and several boys of different ages. It began to feel crowded. There were dogs everywhere, barking and growling and rolling in the dirt.

As evening came on, Konwatieni took her by the hand and led her toward the fire. By now the cook-pot was steaming. Some in the house had eaten already, but others were milling about. It wasn't at all like mealtimes at home in Deerfield, Eunice thought, where everyone sat together on long benches and chairs arranged around a table. There were benches, but no chairs or table; people sat on blankets on the ground wherever they chose to. The food was *kanontara*, just like what they had eaten on the journey through the wilderness. Konwatieni gave Eunice a large wooden spoon for dipping into the pot. But she wasn't hungry at all, and took only a few bites. Afterward Konwatieni showed her to a corner where she could lie down on a mat, with pelts to pull over herself for a covering. It was hard to fall asleep, but finally she did.

She awoke the next morning with a startle; one of the dogs was licking her face. She brushed him aside and looked around. The cabin seemed full of people, most of them up and moving about but a few still asleep. Konwatieni was squatting by the fire, stirring the cook-pot. The girl who was Eunice's age was playing a game with a rope. The rest of the people, she didn't recognize. Again, she felt very much alone and homesick.

She wondered what would happen next. Was she going to stay here with Arakwente and the others? Would anyone be coming to take her back to her own people? When would she see her father and brothers again? Were they in Canada, too?

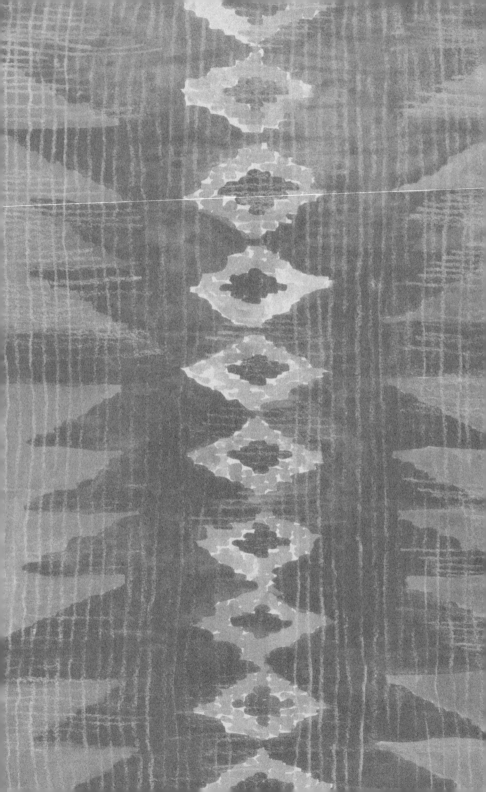

PART TWO

FROM PURITAN
TO MOHAWK

CHAPTER SIX

THE REST OF THE FAMILY

AFTER THE ATTACK, AND AFTER THE FIRES burned down, Deerfield was deserted. The people who had survived and evaded captivity packed up their things and moved out as fast as possible. They rode in carts or on sleds to neighboring towns, where kind friends took them in. Messengers were sent to Boston, the capital city of Massachusetts, to report to the leaders there. The news spread everywhere; people called it a massacre. Fifty people had been killed on that terrible morning.

Soldiers were sent north into the wilderness in the hope of rescuing the captives, but it was too late, and the distance too far. They did come upon the body of Eunice's mother, frozen in the snow but not disturbed. They brought it back and held a proper burial in Deerfield. Her gravestone was carefully engraved to read:

HERE LYETH THE BODY OF MRS. EUNICE
WILLIAMS, THE VIRTUOUS AND DESIRABLE
WIFE OF THE REVEREND MR. JOHN
WILLIAMS, WHO FELL BY THE RAGE OF THE
BARBAROUS ENEMY, MARCH 2, 1704.

Many people in Massachusetts grieved for the mother—and for the daughter, too. They grieved for all the captives, and hoped and prayed for their return. What would it take? Maybe a raid into Canada to find where they were being held? Maybe a plan to help them escape? Maybe a lot of ransom money to pay the Mohawks? Maybe an agreement between the leaders of the French and the English? All these ideas were considered.

Meanwhile, up in Canada, the surviving members of the Williams family were scattered in different locations. Eunice remained in Konwatieni's house, feeling lonely and afraid. Konwatieni and the older daughter, Atsiaha, were nice to her and tried to cheer her up. The little girl—the one who was about her age—kept coming over and smiling at her. She was Onwari, another of the daughters.

They wanted to make her feel like part of their family. They gave her new clothes, including a beautiful tunic made of deerskin and trimmed with brightly colored glass beads. They tried to teach her more of the Mohawk language; she already knew some, but needed to learn more. Konwatieni would point to things around the house and say the words for them: *otsireh* for fire, *oneste* for corn, *ondach* for kettle. Or she would take Eunice outside, point overhead, and say *ienontarah*, their word for sky, and *kara*, for sun. Eunice knew she was supposed to repeat the sounds, and she tried to do it. But in her heart she didn't want to; it was like giving up on being English. She kept thinking of her Deerfield family and wondering where they were. She had no way to know about any of them. Only much later would she learn more.

Samuel, Eunice's oldest brother, was now in Quebec, Canada's capital city. The Indians had turned him over to a Frenchman in exchange for a shipment of wool blankets from Europe. Now he was a servant, a worker on the Frenchman's farm. Of course it felt strange to him, but he was well taken care of, and his new household was welcoming. He learned to speak French and began to make friends with French boys who lived nearby.

The Indians who kept Stephen were Abenakis, a group quite different from the Mohawks. They didn't seem to have any regular home at all. Instead, they traveled here and there through the wilderness, never staying in one place for more than a few days. They hunted deer and moose and fished in the rivers. But their main goal was to catch beavers, whose furry hides could be sold to the French for good money. Wherever they went, they took Stephen with them. One of the older men was his master, but a kind one, more like a teacher than a boss. After the surprise meeting with Eunice that day in the forest, Stephen did not see another white person for months. He became more and more like an Indian, not only in his appearance—clothing and hairstyle—but also in his knowledge of the forest and native ways of living. He learned to track animals, set traps, and build a small shelter. And he could speak the Abenaki language quite well.

Warham, the youngest, was taken straight to a French convent in the city of Montreal. It was somewhat like a church, but also a place where people lived. The grown-ups were all women, Catholic nuns, who prayed a lot and wore long black gowns with white hoods covering their heads. He had never seen anyone dressed that way before, and it seemed strange. There were at least a dozen other children staying there, most of them orphans. Some were French and others were Indians; he was the only English child. At first he felt very lonely. But as the days passed, he got over it. The nuns treated him warmly; they called him *mon cher petit* (meaning, in French, "my little dear"). They mended his clothes, fed him tasty meals, and taught him French songs. After a few months the convent came to seem almost like home to him.

Of course, Eunice's father was in Canada, too. The fact that he was a Puritan minister made him the most important of all the captives. The French governor took him away from the Indians as soon as they reached Canada. The governor had special plans for Reverend Williams, and wanted to keep him under close watch. He was sent to a monastery—a place like a convent but for men (monks), not women. The monks tried very hard to persuade him to convert to Catholicism; what a fine "catch" he would be for their church! They argued with him day after day, and he argued back. Which religion was the true one? That was the question. It went around and around, but neither side gave in.

While this was going on, Reverend Williams grew more and more concerned about his children. From time to time he would get news of them. Apparently, they were all healthy—he was grateful for that—but he also heard things that disturbed him. He heard that they, too, were being urged to convert. A traveler had seen Samuel in the big cathedral in Quebec, and the nuns were teaching Warham their own prayers. He couldn't find out much about Stephen, but Abenakis were said to be Catholic. And as for Eunice, Kahnawàke was known to be a mission, where priests were trying all the time to convert Indians. That made him very worried.

41

CHAPTER SEVEN

THE VISIT

AGAIN AND AGAIN, REVEREND WILLIAMS begged the French governor for a chance to visit Eunice at Kahnawàke. Finally, his wish was granted. By now it was summertime, and traveling was easy. The governor sent a translator with him, so he and the Mohawks would be able to understand each other. They rode on horseback to the edge of the river and went across on a little ferry; the village was on the opposite side. It had been several months since he had last seen Eunice, so he was very eager to get there.

They got off the ferry, walked to the village, and went inside. With the translator's help, he asked some Indian men who were sitting beside the well, "Where is the little English girl? I am her father, and have come to see her." But the men turned away and didn't answer. No one else seemed willing to help, either. He wondered, were the Mohawks hiding her? Had they taken her someplace else? He was beginning to lose hope when suddenly she appeared, running toward him from around a corner and shouting, "Father! Father!" Close behind came Konwatieni, who called to her to turn back. But she kept running and jumped into his arms for a long hug. Konwatieni stood off to one side, her face showing a little scowl.

He put her down and stood back to look her over. Her Indian dress made her seem different; her hair, too, was arranged in a strange way, with long feathered clasps. But yes, she was still *his* daughter, *his* Eunice. And he was still her father. Nothing could change that.

After another minute or two, when the first flush of joy at seeing each other was over, her whole face changed. Her warm smile and bright eyes took on a look of pleading. "Please," she begged him, "please take me away from here. Today, right now, let me go with you, and never come back. Tell them I don't want to stay any longer. They aren't my family; you are. Please, please, please, just tell them." She was in tears; the words came out mixed with her sobs.

Of course, her father wanted the same thing. He turned toward several of the Mohawks standing nearby. They said nothing, but were watching closely. Surely, he thought, they could see how miserable she was, how much she loved him and he loved her. A child should never be left with strangers;

a father could never give up his own child. They had to understand that. But did they? The look in their eyes said no.

Just then Konwatieni moved forward and tried to take Eunice by the arm. But the child shrank away and stood behind her father, clutching his coat. Her sobbing increased, her face became twisted with fear. She spoke to Konwatieni in Mohawk, her voice rising to a wail. Her father could not make sense of the words, but still he understood. She was begging, begging, begging for her release, before any more time had passed.

Eunice turned back to him and spoke in English. "Their houses are dark and dirty," she said, "and I hate their food. They take me to their church on the Sabbath and force me to say their prayers. They are Catholics, father, and they are trying to make me a Catholic, too." For him, this was heart-wrenching, and worst of all was the part about church. *My daughter, a Catholic?* he thought.

He stood up as straight as he could and spoke to the Mohawks in a firm voice. "You *must* let me have my daughter back. Keeping her here is wrong, wicked, *un*-Christian. She is an English girl, a Puritan girl; she can never be one of your people. I'm leaving now and taking her with me." The translator put his words into Mohawk.

He stretched his arm around her and they took a few steps toward the gate. But several Mohawk men quickly blocked their way. Again he stood tall and spoke as firmly as he could. "Remove yourselves! I am Reverend John Williams, and I insist on leaving here with my daughter!" Once more the translator put his words into Mohawk. But the men in front of him folded their arms across their chests and would not budge.

They stood staring at each other for several minutes. Eunice crouched behind her father, crying softly. Then Arakwente appeared, walking rapidly from the opposite end of the village. His manner was solemn, and his eyes showed concern. "My English brother," he said to Reverend Williams through the translator, "do not fear for this child. We love her and will always keep her safe. She belongs with us now. Bid her goodbye, and go in peace."

Her father realized he could do nothing more. He knelt down and offered what little encouragement he could. "I cannot free you from them just now," he said. "But they have promised to look after you, and I believe them. Be sure to pray to *our* God every day, and do not let their Catholic beliefs into your heart. I will come back when I can. And one day you, your brothers, and I will all be together again in our own home." He rose and walked slowly away. When he reached the river, he paused and looked back over his shoulder. His last glimpse of Eunice would stay in his memory forever: a weeping child with hands outstretched, as the gate closed behind him.

CHAPTER EIGHT

LEFT BEHIND

THE WAR OF THE FRENCH AND INDIANS in Canada against the English colonists in Massachusetts went on and on. There were more battles, more surprise raids, and more people captured. But of all those taken—there were hundreds by now—John Williams remained the most famous. People throughout Massachusetts prayed for his return. They prayed also for his children and for the soul of his late wife.

It took two more years, but finally their prayers were answered. The French governor began writing letters to leaders on the English side. He asked about a French pirate called Captain Baptiste, who had been captured by the English several years before. He offered to send Reverend Williams home if the pirate was freed to return to Canada. Ambassadors were sent back and forth to discuss the details; they had long discussions, and finally both sides agreed. It would be a direct swap: Reverend Williams for Captain Baptiste.

Three of the Williams children would be allowed to go home, too. The nuns in the convent said goodbye to little Warham and sent him to join his father. The governor told the French family near Quebec to let Samuel go. And the Indians who held Stephen were given a ransom for his release. Nothing was done about Eunice; she alone would have to remain behind. The Mohawks in Kahnawàke refused to allow her return.

A ship came from Massachusetts for the father and his sons. It had been almost three years since their capture, and they were very glad to be going home at last. If only Eunice were with them, it would have been perfect. Before they went the governor promised Reverend Williams he would speak with the Indians about getting her released. They would have to be patient in the meantime.

They left on a warm fall day. None of them had ever been on an ocean trip before. At first, it went well, but then the weather turned stormy. The wind rose to gale force, and the rain fell in sheets. The ship pitched about on the huge waves, making the children very scared and seasick. One of the sailors lost his balance and fell overboard while trying to lower the sails; there was no way to save him.

It got so bad that the ship seemed about to sink.

Reverend Williams led both crew and passengers in prayer: "Dear Lord," he shouted above the roar of the wind. "Look down on us, your humble servants, in our hour of danger. If it be your will to stop the wind and calm the seas, you can save us from a watery grave." Perhaps he was heard; the storm subsided soon afterward. And the rest of the voyage was easy. Stephen and Samuel spent hour after hour watching for whale spouts; on one afternoon they counted twenty-seven. Dolphins followed in the ship's wake, and seagulls flew back and forth overhead.

After several more days of sailing, the Massachusetts coast finally appeared on the horizon; it was the harbor at Boston. As the ship approached, excited colonists gathered along the shore. They knew what ship this was, and who would be on it. Reverend John Williams was coming home, "redeemed," as they put it, from the French and Indian enemies! The anchor was dropped in deep water and the passengers climbed into small boats to take them to the shore. The colony's governor stepped forward to greet them, and a troop of soldiers fired guns in the air as a salute.

They were taken to the home of Boston's minister, Cotton Mather, where they could stay as long as necessary. Almost at once Reverend Mather began making plans for a special service in his church to celebrate their arrival; the whole town looked forward to it. When the day came, so many people wanted to attend that there weren't enough seats for all of them. Some stood in the aisles, or at the very back, while others were left outside, straining to hear through the open windows. John Williams preached a long sermon, praising God for keeping him and his sons safe while they were captives. He thanked the people of Massachusetts who had prayed so hard for their return. He described what life was like among the French in Canada, and how the wicked priests had tried to convert him. He spoke of Eunice and his failed effort to get her released. He asked everyone to remember her in their prayers. After the service ended there was a procession through the streets. The Williamses rode in the governor's carriage, while the townspeople looked on and cheered.

The family remained in Boston for several months, resting up and making plans for the future. Reverend Williams wanted to get back to Deerfield as soon as possible. But first he needed a new house, because his previous one had burned down in the raid. Some of his neighbors were already back in new houses of their own. The fields were ready for planting, and Granny Hinsdale had reopened the school. Slowly the town was coming back to life, but without the minister, it didn't feel complete.

When spring came, Reverend Williams arranged for the family's return. He hired a carriage, and they traveled along country roads for two long, hot days. When they reached Deerfield they went straight to their new house, which had two floors, two chimneys, lots of windows, and a beautifully carved door. The boys rushed inside and looked around. They would have one room upstairs for themselves. Their father would take the master bedroom. And there was a small room at the rear, to be kept for Eunice when she, too, came home. Two older girls from the town would join the household as servants, and sleep in the attic.

A few months later Reverend Williams went to Connecticut to visit a widow named Abigail Bissell. After a brief courtship he proposed marriage, and she accepted. It was very important to him that his children have a mother's care, and he needed help with running the household, too. The wedding was held in the parlor of the new house; friends and admirers joined them for the occasion. The three Williams boys were pleased and hopeful. Of course, they still missed their mother very much, but they could tell that Abigail would love and look after them.

Everything was back to normal except for the absence of Eunice. Her father kept hoping to hear from the French governor about her, but no word came; it had been more than two years since he'd seen her in the Mohawk village. Then one day a fur trader, back from Canada, stopped in Deerfield for a visit. In the course of his travels, he had been to Kahnawàke, and had asked about Eunice: Was she all right? Would she be sent home soon? The Mohawks said she was in good health and was happy with her life among them. She had gotten used to their ways and didn't want to leave. She loved them, and they loved her with all their hearts. The merchant asked to see her and talk with her directly, but they refused. They told him it was no use anyway, because she had forgotten how to speak English; she was an Indian girl now.

This was the news the trader brought to the Williams family. And it seemed just terrible; they could hardly believe it. *Forgotten how to speak English? An Indian girl now?* Impossible! How could she? Her father went into his study and stayed there, praying by himself for a whole day. The rest of the family tried to get on with regular life, with Mrs. Williams and the servant girls doing women's work in the house and the boys at their chores in the barn. But a deep gloom settled over the entire household.

When the news spread to towns all across Massachusetts, there was more sorrow, more disbelief, more praying. It had been just a short while since the great rejoicing over Reverend Williams's return, but this was so different. That a minister's child born and brought up in good English style should prefer to live with Indians: How strange! How tragic! What could they do to save her?

CHAPTER NINE

BECOMING A
DIFFERENT PERSON

THE TRADER WAS RIGHT. AFTER THE heartbreaking visit with her father left her feeling so abandoned, Eunice had changed a great deal. As the months passed and her memories of Deerfield faded, she began to think of Kahnawàke as home, and Arakwente, Konwatieni, Atsiaha, and Onwari seemed more and more like family.

Step by step, they drew her into their way of life. When spring came, Konwatieni began working in the fields outside the village with other Kahnawàke women, and groups of little girls—including Eunice—tagged along. The women used bent sticks to hoe the ground, which had become lumpy and hard over the winter. When that was done, they built round hills of soil and carefully placed a few kernels of corn in each one. They also planted beans, squash, melons, onions, and pumpkins.

Eunice and the other girls watched from nearby; this was how they learned the skills and duties of a Mohawk woman. Sometimes they would go off to the side and build little hills of their own, using pebbles to "plant" with instead of actual corn.

Another springtime task was collecting sap from the maple trees in the forest. After boiling, the sap would become their sugar; Eunice loved its sweet taste. In the summertime, as the corn and other crops grew tall, there was weeding to do, because the fields had to be kept very clean. If the weather got really hot, water was brought in pails from the river to sprinkle here and there.

In the autumn came the harvest. This was the busiest time of all. The crops had ripened, and now they must be picked and stored for later use. Berries, apples, and other fruits were dried and buried in deep pits lined with tree bark and covered with soil to protect them from the cold. When the corn was ready, the village women went out to the fields as a group. Each one carried a large basket, and worked all day at pulling the cobs from the tall stalks. The little girls would follow a few steps behind to pick up any kernels that might fall to the ground; every bit was precious. Eunice and Onwari walked together, bent low with their eyes peeled. Whenever they found a kernel or two, they let out a happy shout. Konwatieni would turn and smile, and say how well they were doing.

A few days later, the village had a special gathering for stringing all the cobs in long rows. It was a grand occasion; everyone came to help, including the men and boys. When they were done, they grouped together in a field to celebrate. There was a platform where four of the elders sat on a long bench, beating drums and shaking horn rattles filled with seeds. The rest of the villagers, their arms linked, began to dance in a serpentine fashion. The dancers went faster and faster. Eunice, Onwari, and several other children stood to one side, their faces rapt. Finally, when almost everyone seemed exhausted, the elders said it was time to stop. Many of the dancers just fell to the ground and rested where they were.

Later that evening they had a huge meal that lasted for hours. There was so much food—deer meat, fish, squashes and pumpkins, sweet potatoes, acorns, and melons—that Eunice felt stuffed. You were supposed to keep going till nothing was left; that's why it was called an eat-all feast. Everybody slept deeply that night. The next afternoon they gathered once more to finish the harvest by stuffing the stringed cobs into barrels for use later on. Corn was their most important food all year round.

Life for Mohawk children was about more than just work, though; there was also time for fun. Like children everywhere, they played games. There was one, played only by girls, that

Eunice greatly enjoyed. Five or six of them would stand in a circle, tossing a cloth ball the size of an apple. The goal was to keep it in the air as long as possible; if you dropped it or let it fall, you were out.

They also played with the village dogs and horses. The dogs were not very tame; you had to be careful or they would bite. The horses were kept in a little corral with a low fence. Occasionally when the children chased them, they would leap the fence, gallop into the fields, and trample the plants. This was bad, of course, but no one got in trouble. Eunice had noticed right away that Mohawk children were never punished for misbehaving; they were free to do as they pleased. It was so different from Puritan households, where parents often corrected their youngsters with stern words or even a spanking.

During all this work and play, Eunice made new friends. Onwari was becoming like a sister to her because they lived in the same home and were together practically all the time. There were a few other Mohawk girls Eunice felt close to. And also in the village were several other English girls who had been part of the captive group—Martha French, for one. Martha and Eunice had been playmates in Deerfield for as long as they could remember, and had shared the journey to Canada. Occasionally, in the days just after their arrival at Kahnawàke, the two of them would go off to the side

and talk in English about all the things that had happened
to them. But as time passed, they switched to Mohawk and
couldn't remember their first language at all.

It was the custom at Kahnawàke for a captive to be given a
new name—a Mohawk name. This didn't happen right away,
though; you had to get used to Indian life first. For Eunice, it
took about a year and a half.

As the time approached, there was a process she had to go
through, starting with a meeting of members of the Wolf clan.
One autumn afternoon a group of them went to the edge
of the forest, and formed a wide circle. Since it was getting
chilly, everyone wore blankets. A very old woman with snow-
white hair, known as the clan mother, took charge. She sat in
the middle, with Eunice and Konwatieni beside her, and sang
a soft chant. Then she closed her eyes and fell silent for several
minutes, while the name came to her. Later, she would give
it to the elders without telling anyone else. It had to be the
name of someone in the clan who had died recently. The idea
was that the captive would replace that person. The Mohawk
word for this meant "re-quickening"; it was seen almost like
a rebirth.

The main ceremony came a few weeks later. It was
winter now, and the snow lay deep. On the appointed day
Konwatieni woke Eunice up at sunrise, and told her to dress

in her best deerskin tunic and leggings. Her hair was braided and pulled up on top of her head, and she wore a little crown of feathers. When all was ready, the family walked together to a special building, an unusually large longhouse kept for the whole community, right in the village center. Important events were held there, including naming ceremonies.

As the family arrived, a crowd was gathering to watch. One of the village elders, a tall man named Aientas, sat on a stool at the front. A heavy bearskin cape covered his entire body. His face was painted in such vivid colors—red, yellow, white, black—that you could hardly make out his eyes. He wore a leather band around his head with turkey feathers on top. Everyone looked in his direction. He was a seer, able to have visions that guided people in their decisions. He also had special powers to summon the spirits, called orenda, that lived all around in the air, though you couldn't see them. They could make you rich or poor, sick or well, happy or sad. Everyone respected them. It was all part of the Mohawks' religion.

The elder greeted the family with a little nod of recognition. Konwatieni guided Eunice forward in order to present her to the people, the orenda, the four directions of the Earth, and the Mohawk Nation. The people answered with a kind of cheer that showed their approval. The elder stood up, and began to sing in a high, raspy voice. He swayed from side to side, his lips twitched, his eyes bulged. Eunice was scared because she hadn't seen anything like this before, and it didn't seem normal. But Konwatieni whispered in her ear to stay calm; he was just asking the spirits for their blessing. After a few minutes he stopped and stared straight ahead. Then he bent to the ground, picked up a gourd, raised it over his head, and drank something from inside. Finally, he reached for Eunice with both arms and pronounced her new name—A'ongote. Translated into English it meant "she is planted." It must have previously been the name of someone who, like Eunice, had been captured and "planted" in the Nation. From here on the villagers would see her as actually being that person.

When the ceremony was finished Arakwente came to her and bowed low; then Konwatieni and Atsiaha did the same. Onwari laughed and said over and over, "A'ongote, A'ongote, A'ongote." But it wasn't just about having a new name, or being seen as a different person. It meant that she was part of their family—an adopted daughter. It also meant that she would be part of the Wolf Clan. A clan was a large group of cousins and other relatives who would take care of each other in times of need. The Wolf Clan was one of three in the village; the others were the Turtle and the Bear. These same clans were in every Mohawk village, and helped bind the whole tribe together.

As Eunice (or A'ongote) already knew, the Kahnawàke Mohawks were not just part of the longhouse religion, but were also Catholics. Catholic priests had come from France many years before and built a church in the village; Eunice had noticed it the very day she arrived. Konwatieni went there every Sunday for a service they called a mass. Often she took Onwari and Eunice with her.

Konwatieni tried to explain about all these beliefs. There was the Great Spirit, Shonkwaiiatihson, who protected the whole world and commanded the spirits of the forest. He was the most important god in the longhouse religion; Mohawks had looked up to him for thousands of years. The god of the Catholics was different—and, the priests said, the only real one. They claimed that everything the Mohawks believed was false and wicked, and that Shonkwaiiatihson was just a devil. All in all, it seemed very confusing. But Konwatieni said not to worry and not to listen to the priests too much. On Sundays you could pray to the Catholic god, and at other times to Shonkwaiiatihson. Maybe they were even the same, but called by different names.

So now Eunice had to become a Catholic, too. The priests made her start by learning some phrases they called the catechism. She practiced and practiced, and got them memorized. Then it was time to be baptized in the church. This would be done in another ceremony, but nothing like the one in the longhouse. She had already been baptized once before, as a baby in Deerfield, but of course she couldn't remember. Anyway, that was by the Puritans, so the priests said it was worthless.

When the day came, she again had to dress up. But this time she wore a white linen smock and a little silver tiara on her head. She also wore a silver chain around her neck with a medal at the bottom in the shape of a cross. The priests explained that the cross was about Jesus, the son of God, who had come down to Earth long before in order to save Catholics from their sins. Bad men had nailed him to a wooden frame in the shape of a cross, where he had died. But then, by a miracle, he came back to life and went up to heaven. There was a special day called Easter when all Catholics celebrated his resurrection. Eunice wondered whether Jesus was friends with Shonkwaiiatihson in heaven, but she knew not to ask the priests; they would hate the idea.

The church was the largest building in the village. As the family approached, the bell in its tower was ringing loudly to let people know that something important was about to happen. Inside, the main section had rows and rows of wooden benches where people would sit, pray, and listen to the priests. But the most striking thing was a huge table at the front. It was the altar, covered with finely decorated cloth. And hanging just above it was a wooden cross, which was painted gold and even bigger than a person. Along the sides were statues that the priests said were of saints, men who had done wonderful work for God.

Eunice had been in the church many times before, but on this day it seemed more impressive than ever. She trembled a little as Konwatieni took her hand and led her toward the altar, where the priests were waiting. They told her to kneel down and close her eyes while they prayed that God would receive her. They sang a hymn and said more prayers, but since everything was in the Latin language, Eunice couldn't understand any of it. Two women, close friends of Konwatieni's, stood nearby. They would become her godparents, and would be responsible for making sure she was always a good Catholic.

The ceremony finally ended when the priests sprinkled water on her forehead. (Eunice had seen the same thing happen when her baby sister, Jerusha, was baptized in the Puritan church, but by now, that was just a vague memory.) They gave her a name completely different from the one she had been given in the longhouse. It was Marguerite; she thought it sounded pretty. The priests said it had been the name of a French lady who had come to Canada many years before and built a hospital for the Indians. So for the second time she was renamed after someone else. From then on, she would use both names—A'ongote with the village people and Marguerite in the church. She had forgotten all about her original name, Eunice.

This was exactly what John Williams had feared the most—that his own daughter should be joined to the hated Catholics. He wouldn't find out about it for another few months, but when he did, he was terribly upset. It was as bad, he thought, as her becoming an Indian—maybe even worse. Her life would be ruined, her soul would go to hell forever.

CHAPTER TEN

LEARNING THEIR BELIEFS

AS SHE GREW OLDER, A'ONGOTE LEARNED more and more about Mohawk beliefs and customs. It was just part of being there, of belonging to Kahnawàke.

She learned about their history, as told by the old men of the village. Their parents and grandparents had come to Canada quite a few years before, from a homeland far to the south between two enormous lakes. And down there they had been part of a much larger group, the Five Nations of the Iroquois.

Many of the Mohawks who lived in Kahnawàke still had relatives in the homeland, and would go back sometimes for visits. Once when Konwatieni traveled there to see her own mother, she took A'ongote along. Many members of the Wolf Clan came to greet their new cousin. Some brought gifts, including long strings of shell beads called wampum. She could wear these as jewelry, or arrange them in a certain way to convey a message, or use them for trade. One string might be exchanged for a blanket; three strings would be enough for a musket. Konwatieni told A'ongote to save hers for the future, when she would need them more. So after they returned home, she kept them in a secret hiding place, a hole inside a tree in the forest.

One morning, Aientas, the village elder who had performed A'ongote's naming ceremony some years before, came to see her in her family's home. He wanted, he said, to tell her about the ancient beginnings of their people—before Canada, before the homeland, before there was anything like the present. He said it would take three days to tell the whole story. When she learned it, she would be cleansed of her English blood, and her soul would be truly Mohawk.

On the first day he took her deep into the forest. They sat together under a huge oak tree where, he said, the spirits would come to help him remember the story. Then he began to tell her about Sky Woman and the start of the Earth.

"Long, long ago, there was no land and no people, just water everywhere. High above was a sky world, where a spirit creature named Sky Woman lived with her husband. Sky Woman became pregnant, but her husband thought it was not his child, and felt jealous. He told her to uproot a tree and make a hole in the clouds. When she did that, he pushed her through the hole. She fell down, down, down, for what seemed like many days. Finally, just as she was about to touch the water, a flock of geese came to catch her on their wings. Then Turtle swam up and said she could climb on his broad back. But she needed earth in order to live properly. Beaver and Otter dove to the sea bottom to get mud for her, but died trying. Muskrat brought enough mud for her to make a home on Turtle's back; then he, too, died. This was the start of the Earth. After some time Sky Woman's baby was born—a daughter. And when the daughter was grown, she became pregnant with twin sons; one was good, the other evil. The good twin was born in the normal way, but the evil one insisted on coming out through his mother's armpit, which killed her. From her body grew corn, beans, tobacco, and squash, and from her head came the moon. Sky Woman tried to make her grandsons, the twins, behave. But the evil twin wouldn't listen and kept fighting his brother. Eventually the good twin won, and banished the evil one to a cave. The good twin created humans, the animals of the forest, and corn and other plants for food. The evil twin stayed in his cave, but could still send out wicked spirits to cause harm."

That was the first day's story. A'ongote was fascinated, but also scared. She wondered, *What if the bad twin comes to the village? What will he look like? How will I recognize him?*

The next day Aientas came again and took her to the same great tree. When they sat down, she heard a strange sound, a kind of rustling directly overhead. *Perhaps it's an orenda*, she thought, but she was afraid to look. Then Aientas told her about the very first Mohawks.

"After the good twin left, humans divided themselves into nations. One nation lived on the edge of the Earth where the sun set, but the land was poor and many people were dying. Their leader was Gaihonariosk, a woman of great knowledge and skill. She said they must travel to the east to have a better life. She led them on a long journey across the whole of the Earth, climbing mountains, crossing deserts, fording rivers. They endured storms, floods, droughts, and attacks by evil spirits. And still they wandered, looking for the right place. After many hardships, they reached the shore of a great lake where the land seemed good. They stayed for a number of years, but the winters were bitterly cold and the growing season was too short for a proper harvest, so Gaihonariosk said they must move once more. She led them south till they reached a place that was green, well watered and not too cold, and had good soil for growing their crops. At last they could put down their burdens and start living in a settled way. Gaihonariosk was old by then, but before she died she divided the fields among all the people. They planted corn, and built villages, and it became their homeland."

That was the second day's story; A'ongote thought it was wonderful. She wished she had met Gaihonariosk. *What a brave woman!* she thought. *If only I could be like Gaihonariosk when I grow up.*

On the third day, when Aientas came, A'ongote was waiting. They walked together to the same tree and Aientas started in on the final story.

"Having settled in their own place, the Mohawks grew and prospered. But there was trouble with their neighbors. Several nations inhabited the same region, and fighting broke out among them. As the years passed, things grew worse and worse. Warfare came to seem normal, and many brave warriors were killed. The land itself seemed bloodied, and their corn withered and died because no one looked after it.

"Then a child named Skennenrahawi was born in a village far to the north. Even from his earliest years he seemed especially generous, wise, and strong. When he was grown he set out on a journey in a white canoe. He crossed a great lake and found hunters whose village had been destroyed. They described to him their constant warfare, killing, even cannibalism. Skennenrahawi told them that the Great Spirit had sent him to teach them the ways of peace. They listened, but did not at first agree.

"Skennenrahawi continued on his journey, and met a woman named Djigonsasa, the Mother of Nations, who fed warriors along the road. She accepted his message, the first to do so. He walked some more and came to a longhouse, where a cannibal was eating a meal of human flesh. He persuaded the cannibal to stop, and gave him the name Hiawatha. From then on the two walked together. Hiawatha's family went with them. But as they traveled east, they came upon a powerful witch with snakes in his hair named Tadadaho. The witch rejected their message and used magic to kill Hiawatha's seven daughters.

"Grieving his loss, Hiawatha wandered by himself and came to the Mohawks. He showed them the proper way to deliver messages and use wampum. Then he went further and again met Skennenrahawi, who comforted him and relieved his sorrow. Together they created a special ceremony of condolence, as well as a peace hymn. One after another, the nations accepted their message.

"Led by Skennenrahawi, the nations marched in procession to Tadadaho, singing the peace hymn. Tadadaho's wicked heart was softened, and he combed the snakes out of his hair. Now all the nations were joined as one great family. And ever since they have remained at peace with each other. Even today their chiefs meet in council and agree together. And Skennenrahawi is remembered by everyone as the Great Peacemaker."

Aientas rose and motioned for A'ongote to follow him back to the village. As they walked, she thought about Skennenrahawi—what a great man he was, and how lucky the nations were that he had lived among them.

After the three days of stories, A'ongote thought it was over. But the next week Aientas came back to her house and said she had even more to learn—about creatures, and souls, and the world of spirits. So they went again to sit under the great oak tree.

Almost immediately Aientas began speaking once more. He told A'ongote about the animals of the forest and how they are the brothers and sisters of humans. He described the world of spirits, where thoughts and actions are the same. He explained the duties of men and women, the skills needed to keep families safe, and important customs of the whole community. Then he paused and looked up toward the top of the tree. After several minutes he resumed, turning now to the question of souls.

"Every person has a soul that is very important to the right way of living. The soul is the source of thoughts, of feelings, and especially of wishes and desires. It moves about constantly, and directs a person's energy toward various goals. It is independent of the body; it can go on long journeys while the body remains still. It flies through the air, passes over seas, and can enter the most tightly enclosed places.

"Also, the soul can speak to the orenda, the spiritual force within all things, and reveal what a person should do. This happens mostly during sleep, in dreams. A dream is a command from the soul, and should always be obeyed. If, for example, a man dreams of meat roasting over a fire, he must, upon waking, be served a well-cooked meal. Or, if he dreams of falling sick, he will awake with a fever and may fear for his life. For these reasons it is necessary to pay the closest attention to dreams, and to act always in accord with them.

"After the death of the body, the soul departs for its own country beyond the heavens. The route is along the Star Path far above the clouds. It ends in a great and beautiful land, with a huge and colorfully decorated longhouse at the center. As the souls approach, sounds of lovely chanting and the scent of delicious foods come toward them. Other souls, already present, rush out to escort them the rest of the way. Once inside the longhouse, they see dancing and feasting, and are invited to join in. From that point forward, they feel no worry or anger or hungry desire; instead, there is only joy."

Finally, Aientas fell silent. He had now given A'ongote all the knowledge she needed to be fully accepted as a Mohawk. After another minute or two, he rose from his place under the tree and vanished into the woods.

A'ongote knew the way home by now, and she walked back by herself. She thought about all she had heard. She wondered especially about her own soul. How, exactly, would she know it? Was it really part of her? Could it be traveling right now to some place she'd never seen? These questions kept going around and around in her mind. Would she ever have the answers?

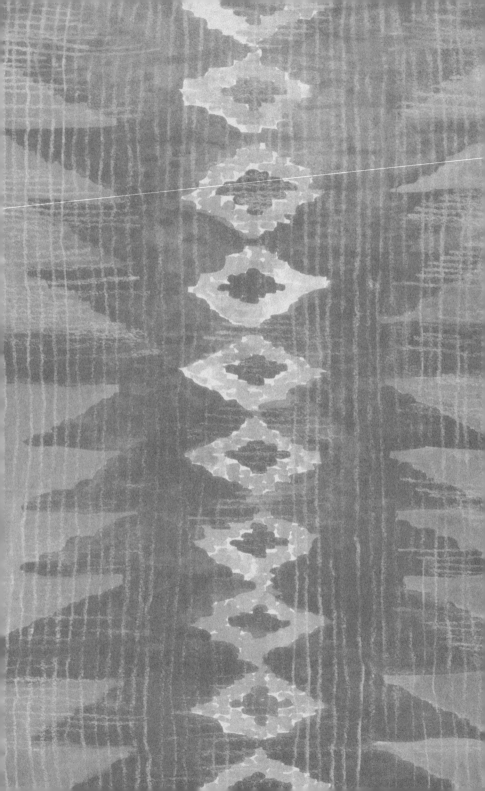

PART THREE

MOHAWK GIRL

CHAPTER ELEVEN

TRAGEDY STRIKES

FOR THE NEXT FEW YEARS, A'ONGOTE'S life followed a quiet track. She had become like any other Kahnawàke girl, enjoying her family, helping out in the longhouse and the fields, playing with her friends.

She had no way to know how hard John Williams and many others among the English were trying to reach out and bring her back to Massachusetts. Letters were sent to the French governor, and merchants who went to Canada always asked about her. But the Mohawks were more determined than ever to keep her as one of their own, so they didn't answer. And she had no wish to leave.

Her life from day to day was spent mostly with the women and girls. Weeks went by when the men of the village were gone—on the winter hunt, for example, or to make more raids against the English. At such times she missed Arakwente; after all, he had been her first caretaker among the Mohawks. Most of the time, of course, he was in the village. He never stayed overnight with Konwatieni and the rest of the family because it was the custom for Mohawk men to live at the homes of their mothers even after they married. But he came every day to visit, and to make sure everything was all right.

In fact, A'ongote could see that the women ran the village. The cabins belonged to them, and the fields too; they were in charge of almost all property. Children belonged to the mother's family, not the father's. The leaders of the village government—the chiefs—were men, but the women held meetings of their own to give their opinions. On some matters, such as when to go to war or what to do with captives, they were the ones to decide. Women even chose the chiefs. A'ongote now understood that it was Konwatieni, not Arakwente, who had adopted her into their family. If she remembered anything from her earliest years, she might have realized that women had a more important role among the Mohawks than they did among the Massachusetts Puritans.

Kahnawàke women were also important as traders at local markets. From time to time they would go into Montreal, a large French town just across the river, with furs, corn, or deer hides to exchange with French merchants for iron pots, woolen blankets, and glass beads. Konwatieni was one of the women who did this. And it was she who, without knowing it, brought tragedy upon the village. On a hot summer day, while walking through the Montreal market, she passed a sailor fresh off a boat from France. He stopped, turned, and begged her for a drink of water. She let him take a few gulps from a flask she was carrying and then hurried on. But the sailor was ill with smallpox, the most terrible disease in those days. So a bit later, when she drank from the same flask, she, too, became infected. She returned to the village as usual, suspecting nothing because the symptoms didn't develop right away. But five days afterward she awoke feeling sick, and soon her face and body were covered with smallpox sores. By this time, she had unknowingly infected some of her family and neighbors. It didn't take much to pass on the virus—just the touch of a hand, a cough, a sneeze.

The others knew what Konwatieni's illness was right away, because Indian people had been struck by smallpox many times before. The virus had come with the first colonists from Europe, where countless people had died from it over the centuries. Those colonists had given it to the Indians, and then it spread in great waves called epidemics all across America. It seemed to affect Indians even worse than white people; they got sicker and died faster. Whole villages could be wiped out in just a few months. Kahnawàke had already suffered through two previous epidemics.

So when Konwatieni got the sores, everyone was frightened. Still, they had a plan. They took her out of her own house to another one that was kept especially for sick people; it was the Mohawk version of a hospital. There, they would try to look after her while having as little direct contact with her as possible.

Arakwente came every day, stood at the door, called softly to her, and left food cooked at his mother's house. One of Konwatieni's sisters who was skilled at nursing came too; she brought clean clothes and coverings for the sores. The children—Onwari, Atsiaha, and A'ongote—were told to stay away. The most they could do was go to the church and pray to Jesus, or call on the spirits to make her well.

Just a few days later the sores began to appear on Onwari, at first on her chest and neck, then everywhere. She was put in the hospital house alongside her mother. Both of them were very sick. One minute they were hot with fever, the next they were shivering with chills. The sores got worse; sometimes blood ran out of them. An old woman, a Mohawk healer, came to help. She knew about using herbs and other plants as a cure. A'ongote was very worried and sad. Onwari was her best friend, and Konwatieni was her mother. There were some days when A'ongote lay in the cabin and cried for hours.

The best hope for a cure was what the villagers called the sweathouse. This was a little hut covered with straw mats on the outside. There were no windows, just a tiny door you could barely crawl through. Inside, it was dark and very hot. In the center there was a pile of steaming rocks that had been heated in a fire. The idea was to make the sick person sweat a lot so the disease would come out through the pores of their skin. Konwatieni and Onwari went there several times every day. Once A'ongote peeked through the door and could see how uncomfortable they were. She felt very sorry for them, but everyone said it would help them fight the disease.

Finally, after two weeks, Onwari began to get better. Her fever dropped and the sores dried up, although they would leave her with a lot of ugly scars. It went more slowly with Konwatieni, but eventually she, too, recovered. Everyone in the household was relieved. Luckily, Atsiaha and A'ongote continued to be well.

By now, though, smallpox was running throughout the village. Dozens of people were infected, then hundreds; there seemed to be no way of stopping its spread. One of the priests came down with it and died after three days. They had to set aside two more longhouses as hospitals. As the number of deaths increased, there were funerals constantly.

Arakwente was in charge of organizing many of the funerals. He was so strong and smart that people thought he would not get infected. But finally he did. The sores appeared and covered his body, just as with all the other cases. He went to the hospital house, and from there to the sweathouse. A'ongote watched him from a distance, and felt very worried. Early one morning while A'ongote was still asleep, Konwatieni came in from outside, weeping and calling out, "My husband is gone! My husband is gone!" A'ongote ran to her for a tight hug, and their tears mixed together. Arakwente had died during the night.

Now Arakwente would have his own funeral. And because he had been an important man, it was a major event. To begin, a large group gathered at his mother's cabin. Some cut their hair to show their grief.

Eventually they went to the burial place, where a pit had been dug for the body. They put in some wampum, some clothes, some food, and other things the soul would need on its journey. When the pit had been closed, they returned to their homes.

That night the entire village gathered for a feast in Arakwente's honor. They roasted a deer over a huge open fire. They sang more dirges and some gave long speeches about the dead man's strength and courage. One of the speakers talked about Arakwente's part in the Deerfield raid, his bravery in the moment of attack, and his care of the prisoners on the return journey to Canada. A'ongote, sitting by the fire with the rest of the family, covered her eyes and wept.

This was only the start of the mourning, especially for Konwatieni. For ten days she remained in the house, in keeping with the Mohawk custom. On the tenth day she began to withdraw from mourning.

A'ongote watched from a careful distance. She, too, was grief-stricken, but she knew she must keep to herself. Sometimes in the evenings, she would go into the woods and find the great oak tree where Aientas had told her the story of their people. Under the tree, she would think about all that Arakwente had done for her, starting with the journey through the wilderness. As had happened before, she thought she saw spirits fluttering in the branches overhead, and she called on them to heal her sorrow. "Oh, kind spirits," she cried in Mohawk, "give my father an easy passage to the country of souls, and let me see him there someday."

In fact, it was the second time she had lost a father. After so many years, she couldn't remember the first one. But there were moments when the image of a tall man—with pale skin, a long face, and sorrowful eyes—came suddenly into her mind. It was strange and confusing. She wondered, was it a vision sent by her soul? Was it a dream she must obey?

CHAPTER TWELVE

OTHER WORLDS

FINALLY, THE SMALLPOX EPIDEMIC ENDED, and there were no more funerals. Many people—men, women, children—had died, and whole families had been broken apart. It was the custom for a widow to marry again with someone else from her late husband's family. So, the next year Konwatieni became the wife of Arakwente's younger brother, Atonnion. He seemed like a good man, skilled at hunting and traveling by canoe. As A'ongote would soon find out, he was also kind to children.

Slowly life in the village went back to normal. When spring came, A'ongote joined Konwatieni and other women in preparing the fields for planting. But there were worries, too. It was 1711—seven years after the Deerfield raid—and the war against the English had flared up again.

As summer began, a stranger arrived in the village, a young Mohawk warrior from the homeland named Arosen. He carried long belts made of wampum to give as a sign of respect and friendship. After all, the people of the homeland and the people of Kahnawàke were closely related. Arosen had a secret message to present. The homeland Mohawks were allies of the English; they wanted their "brothers and sisters" in Kahnawàke to switch sides and join them in fighting the French. It was a difficult question. The village chiefs held long discussions, trying to decide the best plan.

While all this was going on, Arosen stayed in Konwatieni's house as a guest, so he and A'ongote became friends. She was fifteen now, about to go through an important step that would change her life. When it was time, the family once again went to the big longhouse for a special ceremony. And once again Aientas took charge. He was in the same costume as before, a bearskin robe and feathered headband, with lots of face paint. He danced and sang while A'ongote sat on the ground in front of him. Finally, he stopped, poured liquid from a gourd, and said that from now on she would have another name, Gannenstenhawi. Translated into English, it meant "she brings in corn." Since farming corn was the main job of all Kahnawàke women, this new name told everyone to treat her as an adult. Arosen was present for the ceremony and knew all about it because they did the same thing for teenage girls in the homeland. When it was over, he came up to congratulate A'ongote (now Gannenstenhawi), kissing her on both cheeks. He noticed how fine she looked in her deerskin tunic and her hair decorated with pink flowers.

After several days, the village chiefs decided not to join the other Mohawks as allies of the English. They would continue to fight on the side of the French, but would try to avoid direct battles against any of the homeland people. With that decided, Arosen had to leave to give the news to his own chiefs. This was risky because the French had heard about his visit to the village and wanted to capture him; to them, he was a spy. They sent soldiers into the forest to lie in wait along the path until he passed by. But instead, when night fell, he swam across the river beside the village, took a different route home, and escaped.

When fall came, Konwatieni and Atonnion planned a journey for the whole family back to the homeland. It had been several years since any of them had visited there. At first they traveled on a river going south. But the last part was many miles of walking through the forest. As big and strong as she now was, Gannenstenhawi didn't mind at all. She and Onwari were often in the lead, calling to the others behind. Finally, they reached a large Mohawk town and stopped; this was where their relatives in the Wolf Clan lived.

Konwatieni introduced Atonnion to the clan elders. For some minutes, he stood silently before them. Then there was a special ceremony of welcome, with speeches and chanting and the exchange of gifts. All the relatives had put on their best clothing—deerskin leggings and tunics that were painted in bright colors and decorated with beaded designs. It was a joyous time. Gannenstenhawi and Onwari and their girl cousins joined hands and danced together. This was Gannenstenhawi's family, these were her people; she had never felt happier.

But the journey was only half done. After they left the homeland, they walked back to the same river, got into their canoes, and went on farther south. They were headed to Albany, the capital of the English colony called New York. Gannenstenhawi and Onwari rode in a canoe with two of their cousins. Other cousins were in other canoes—it was a big group going together. One of the canoes was loaded high with pelts (animal furs) to be offered in trade. The travel was difficult; tree branches hung out over the water, and rocks were hidden under the surface. Everyone, including the girls, had to paddle hard and be careful not to hit anything. By the time they reached Albany, Gannenstenhawi was exhausted.

But when she saw the town, she was amazed. It had many large houses made of wood and brick, all of them very different from the longhouses of Kahnawàke. A wide street paved with stones went uphill from the river. At its top stood an open marketplace where dozens of people were milling about and shouting to each other in a language Gannenstenhawi couldn't understand. The men wore heavy trousers, long coats, and fur hats. Many had bushy beards, which made them seem rather scary to the Indian girls. The women were in long skirts and wore lacy bonnets on their heads.

Konwatieni explained that these were Dutch people, not the same as the French and English, but not so different, either. The members of all three groups had very pale skins—that was obvious right away—and strange customs like sometimes beating children with a stick and wearing heavy clothes even in the summertime. All of them had come across the sea in wooden boats that were much bigger than any canoe, Konwatieni said. They had taken land from the Indians, cut down the forests, and built towns like this one in their own style. Most were farmers who lived out in the countryside, but the ones at the market were merchants trading goods.

Gannenstenhawi and her family stood on one side of the market and watched. It was unpleasant: so loud, so rough, so disorganized. *These people*, Gannenstenhawi thought, *don't act with respect!* After several minutes Atonnion turned away.

It was time for them to leave, he said. They would come back the next day with their load of pelts after spending the night in the Indian House, a place that was kept especially for native people who had come to trade.

They walked back down the street, almost to the shore. They found the Indian House, a low, wide cabin with a flat roof and rickety walls that seemed about to buckle. It was owned by the Albany merchants, but no one was taking proper care of it. Inside, at least a dozen men were laying mats on the floor. They were from different places, and looked different, and spoke different languages, but all of them were Indians who had come to trade goods. Konwatieni led the way to a vacant corner where the family would have enough room to lie down.

The next morning they were up early and back in the market, this time with their pelts. Atonnion motioned to one of the merchants, who walked over and began examining what they had brought. He had a red face and a big beard that went down over his chest. He said something that sounded mean and spat on the ground. But he and Atonnion started talking—or at least gesturing—to each other. They needed to reach an agreement on how much the man should pay for the pelts.

Gannenstenhawi could see that it would take a long time, so she took Onwari by the hand and, together, they wandered off. Then, on the far side of the market, they came upon something else. A crowd had formed a circle around three very dark-skinned young women. The women were naked except for a small cloth around their hips. Their eyes darted nervously about. A large man stood alongside them, poking at them and calling out in a loud voice. Gannenstenhawi thought he was asking the crowd for something. After a few minutes, another man stepped forward with a handful of silver coins. He gave them to the first man and grabbed the arm of one of the women. She shrieked and tried to shake him off. But the first man grabbed her, too, and together they wrestled her to the ground.

Gannenstenhawi and Onwari felt confused and upset by what they were seeing. Just then Konwatieni walked up from behind. Gannenstenhawi, close to tears, turned and asked her, "What is happening to this woman? Why are the men fighting her? Why is she here at all?" Konwatieni knew the answer, but she paused to find the right words. "The woman comes from a place called Africa, where everyone has black skin. The white people go in their big boats and kidnap them and bring them here. They are sold as property, like cows or pigs, and are made to work very hard. That is what's happening here in the market, the buying and selling of slaves." Gannenstenhawi felt even worse for the poor woman, who was now being dragged off to her new owner's carriage. She couldn't bear to watch anymore and let Konwatieni lead her quickly away, with Onwari following a few paces behind.

When they got back to the other side of the market, they found Atonnion finishing his bargain with the Dutch merchant. The merchant would take all the pelts and in exchange would give them five large packets of cloth that had been made in his home country, along with several iron pots and two bagfuls of glass beads. Atonnion seemed pleased. The cloth would be very useful in Kahnawàke. Some of it they would keep for themselves, and the rest they would sell. The pots could be broken apart and, together with the beads, used in making jewelry. Mohawk people, especially the leaders, wore jewelry as a mark of honor.

Once the exchange had been made, Gannenstenhawi and her family had to leave Albany in a hurry because winter was beginning now. As they walked back through the woods to the river, where their canoes had been left, snow was falling in large, wet flakes. Soon the ground was covered, and Atonnion said they should stop. He took out a little sack of leather strands he had brought from the village and began cutting branches from nearby trees. By weaving the strands between the branches, he was able to make snowshoes, which would make their travel much easier. He worked quickly, and Konwatieni helped him. After a couple of hours, there were snowshoes for all of them, but the delay meant they had to sleep in the woods that night while the snow kept falling. The next afternoon, they reached the river, found their canoes, got back on the water, and started northward toward home.

For two days everything went smoothly. The snow finally stopped and the sun came out; the air seemed almost warm. They had four canoes, which were strung out in a line heading upriver. Gannenstenhawi and Onwari sat at the front of the first one, singing to each other. Everyone was happy, thinking about getting back to the village. But a surprise awaited them.

As they went around a sharp bend in the river, Gannenstenhawi noticed something strange. The bushes along the shore were moving; she thought that men might be hiding behind them. She called to Atonnion, to let him know. But he was where he couldn't see the bushes, and he said not to worry. They had gone just a little farther when suddenly several French soldiers jumped out and rushed toward them, with muskets raised. The soldiers called to them to stop and bring their canoes ashore, an order that could not be refused. They did as they were told and climbed out onto a little beach, where they were forced to show the goods they were carrying home—the cloth, the iron pots, the beads. The soldiers then knew they had been at the Albany market, which was against the laws of Canada. Indians living there, including the people of Kahnawàke, were supposed to trade only with the French.

The soldiers piled the goods behind some rocks bordering the water and walked the whole family to a small hut nearby. They pushed everyone in, shouting and making a lot of angry gestures. They beat Atonnion with sticks till he fell on the floor, blood oozing from his head. Konwatieni and Atsiaha knelt beside him, begging the soldiers to stop. Gannenstenhawi and Onwari crouched in a corner, badly frightened. But just at that moment a group of Indian warriors came running out of the forest and surrounded the hut, firing their muskets as a warning; now it was the soldiers' turn to be surprised. With no chance of fighting back, they laid down their arms and surrendered. The Indians tied them up and locked them in their own hut. Suddenly, Gannenstenhawi's family was free!

They thanked their rescuers very warmly. Konwatieni put cloths on Atonnion's head as a bandage; luckily, his wound wasn't as bad as it had seemed. Then they ran back to their canoes, gathered up their trade goods, and set off on the river again; they needed to move fast in case other French soldiers learned what had happened and tried to come after them. When night fell, they kept going; the moon was full, and they could follow the route without difficulty. They did stop for a few hours of sleep in a small meadow by the shore, but got back on the water early the next morning. Soon they could see the longhouses of Kahnawàke in the distance. Around noon they reached the riverbank in front of the village gate. Friends watching from inside saw them coming and ran out to greet them.

They were home at last. What a long journey it had been!

CHAPTER THIRTEEN

A WINTER HUNT

BY NOW THE WINTER WAS WELL UNDER WAY.
In Kahnawàke, a group of a dozen or so men was getting ready
for the annual hunt. They cleaned their muskets, gathered
their warmest garments (heavy cloaks lined with beaver fur,
leggings made of moose hide), repaired old snowshoes or
made new ones, and filled large basketlike packs with corn
from the previous harvest. They hoped to find game—moose,
deer, bear, caribou—to kill, skin, and carry home to the
village. Once thoroughly dried, the meat from these animals
could be stored and eaten throughout the lean months of
spring and early summer.

Gannenstenhawi watched these preparations with interest.
Of course she had seen it all in previous years, but this time
there was a difference. She would herself be having a part in

the hunt. It was customary for some of the village women to go along as helpers. They carried supplies on the way out, cooked meals for the group at overnight camps, and helped prepare the animals that had been killed. Finally, they would shoulder—together with the hunters—the heavy burdens of the trip home.

The group would include two or three elders wise in the ways of the forest, several young men eager to show their skill, and a few boys going for the first time. Gannenstenhawi was one of five women.

When all was in readiness, the group's leader went to meet with Aientas. He would advise them where to go to find animals. The hunters sat in a circle around him, while he puffed vigorously on a long pipe made of polished stone. The smoke curled up and hovered over him. It seemed to take the shape of an arrow, pointing to the west. "That," he said, "is the direction you must travel." The others nodded, and one asked what animals they would find. Aientas set the pipe aside, rose to his feet, closed his eyes, and began a song to the orenda. "Spirits of the forest," he sang, "give guidance to these brave hunters." His body trembled and he cried out as if in pain; the spirits were entering his soul. Finally, he announced a vision: "I see a valley filled with oak trees, and a lake at the bottom, and three big moose lapping water at the shore." The hunters thanked him and turned their faces toward the sun that was just about to set on the western horizon. Without another word, they formed a line to begin their journey. Gannenstenhawi and the other women were at the rear. Several of the village dogs ambled alongside, barking loudly; they would be useful in tracking the animals.

The snow was deep as they set out; everyone wore snowshoes. Within another hour it was completely dark, so they stopped to camp beside a frozen stream. They made a supper of *kanontara* and got ready to sleep in a grove of fir trees. They cleared the ground of snow, and lay down bunched together under piles of bearskins. The dogs, too, cuddled close. Still, Gannenstenhawi thought she had never felt such cold; she shivered uncontrollably as the night wore on. She was so glad when at last morning came and they could start a fire to warm themselves.

It was like this every day for the next week: hours and hours of walking, meals, making camp, trying to sleep in the frigid night. They saw lots of animal tracks in the snow, but no actual game. Several times the dogs barked excitedly and ran off to give chase. But they always came back with their tongues hanging out, breathing hard and looking disappointed. Then, near the end of the seventh day, one of the leaders walking in front suddenly motioned to everyone to stop and be still. He had heard, faint and far ahead, a moose call. It was getting too dark to proceed farther, so they made another camp and waited for morning.

At sunup, they rose quickly and resumed their walking. They heard more moose calls, which grew louder and louder as they went. At noontime they reached the top of a hill where they could look down into a broad valley. In the middle was a lake, mostly frozen and gleaming white under the sun. At one corner, a stream ran out; there, the ice had melted and the water flowed free. Three moose were bent over, drinking deeply.

The leaders gave a signal and the hunters ran toward the lake, the dogs leaping out ahead. The moose heard them coming and tried to escape across the ice. But because it was slippery, they couldn't go fast. The hunters fired their muskets, and the biggest moose was hit in the shoulder. He fell, then staggered back up as the dogs surrounded him, nipping at his heels. He tried to kick them away, but the hunters closed in and shot some more, and it was the end of him. Gannenstenhawi, with the other women, watched from a rocky ledge on the side of the hill. It was the first time she had seen an animal killed, and she felt sad for the moose, but knew the villagers depended on getting food this way.

After pausing to catch their breath, the hunters formed a circle around the moose's body, pushed the dogs aside, and knelt in the snow. One of the leaders began a chant, and after a minute the others joined in. Gannenstenhawi strained to hear as the words floated up from the valley below. "Oh, fine moose, we kneel before you now in order to give thanks," the hunters sang. "We honor your strength and courage. You and your brothers rule the forest, and are beloved of the spirits. You give the flesh of your bodies to humans when winter comes and our corn is gone, and there is nothing left to eat. May your soul enjoy forever the glory of your sacrifice." As they stood up with their heads still bowed, Gannenstenhawi thought she saw tears on the faces of two or three.

At last it was time to prepare the moose's body for the trip back to the village. The same leader motioned to the women on the ledge to come down. They formed a line; because she was the youngest, Gannenstenhawi walked at the rear. They, too, must honor the dead animal, so each one bowed low as she approached.

The women brought large knives to distribute among the group. And so the carving began with all taking part, the women alongside the men. They carefully removed the hide and set it to one side; someday it could be made into a robe. They built several large racks from tree branches, cut the moose flesh into strips, and laid those out to dry. It took two full days. Then, when all was ready, they wrapped the dried meat in cloth they had brought from the village, and put it in their packs. By now it was late in the afternoon, and the work had exhausted them. The men lay down and napped, but the women still had to make the evening meal. Gannenstenhawi trudged off to gather wood for a fire while the others prepared a portion of meat for roasting. When it was ready they ate in silence, and afterward everyone went right to sleep.

In the middle of the night Gannenstenhawi had a vivid dream. She was lost in a thick forest, running this way and that. As time passed, she became tired and scared; how would she find her way out? She sat down and began to weep. Suddenly a young moose appeared and stopped in front of her. She shrank away in fear, but the moose just looked at her. After a minute he turned and began to move forward; somehow, she knew she must follow. They walked for miles, with the moose in the lead. Eventually they came to an open field; on the other side were the longhouses of a beautiful village. She was safe! The moose had guided her! How could she thank him? No longer afraid, she ran to stroke the hair on his long neck. But as she approached, he turned into a man. Again she shrank away, but the man gave her a warm smile. And then he vanished into the air.

The next morning when the sun rose and everyone woke up, she told the dream to an older woman who was lying next to her. Called Tewennatetha, she was "wise," people said, because she could talk to the orenda and learn their wishes. Tewennatetha listened intently to the dream and then moved her face close to Gannenstenhawi's. "Your dream is very important," she said solemnly. "Soon you will meet someone who will lead you toward the future." Gannenstenhawi could not imagine what she meant, but kept the thought in her mind as they all got ready to break camp.

The trip back to the village was difficult. Snow was falling again, and the air felt colder than ever. The packs they carried, now loaded with moose meat, were much heavier than before. One of the men had fallen ill and could scarcely walk; his companions made a litter from fallen tree branches for carrying him. The going was so slow that Gannenstenhawi thought it might take weeks to get home. But on the second day the sky cleared and the weather got much warmer. It felt like spring! Their spirits rose and their pace quickened.

By now they were on a well-known trail connecting Indian villages in Canada with regions to the south and west. As they trudged along, they came upon the snowshoe prints of other travelers up ahead. The leaders ordered a stop to consider what this meant. There were different possibilities, different dangers. Perhaps they would meet Indian enemies of Kahnawàke; there might even be an ambush. Or French and English soldiers using the same trail might stop them from going on. Either way, they had to be prepared. The leaders decided they should travel in a special formation. Several of the younger men would sneak out in front to scout for signs of suspicious activity. The rest would be divided into two groups, with one half going to the left of the trail, the other to the right. Everyone would walk in a crouched position, careful to make as little sound as possible. Gannenstenhawi felt frightened; she remembered what had happened a few months before, on the journey home from Albany. She stayed near wise old Tewennatetha, who tried to reassure her.

Suddenly the scouts ran back. Up ahead, they had seen several Indians gathered around a campfire. This didn't sound dangerous, so everyone relaxed. When they got close, they saw not enemies, but friends from the homeland. Gannenstenhawi recognized one right away: Arosen, the young warrior who had come to the village and stayed in her family's house the summer before. He recognized her, too, and gave her a warm smile.

Now there were greetings all around. Arosen introduced his father and mother and told the hunters that they wished to go to Kahnawàke to live. They had become Catholics and been baptized by priests who'd visited the homeland. They knew that Kahnawàke had a real church, with a mass every week. Arosen, too, hoped to be baptized someday. But most of their neighbors in the homeland hated Catholics and saw them as traitors to Shonkwaiiatihson and the orenda. It would be better for them to go where they were welcome and could practice the religion they preferred.

Then the group went on, all traveling together. The rest of the journey back took another week, but with spring coming, at least the daytime was mild. Some of the streams they came to were flowing very fast because of all the melting snow, and getting to the other side was hard. Once, while trying to cross on a fallen tree trunk, Gannenstenhawi lost her balance and fell into the water. She still didn't know how to swim, and it looked as if she might be swept away. Luckily, Arosen was just behind her. He jumped in, paddled out to where she was floundering about, and pulled her to safety. They were both soaked, of course, and had to take time to dry off in the sun. Gannenstenhawi struggled with the fear she had felt—it had been such a narrow escape. Tewennatetha came over and urged her to be brave about it, because that was the Mohawk way.

What was left when her fear had passed was deep gratitude toward Arosen—gratitude and something more. She said nothing to anyone, but her feelings for him were very strong.

CHAPTER FOURTEEN

A MARRIAGE

IN THE VILLAGE, PEOPLE WERE WAITING for the hunters to return. They had been gone for a long time; why weren't they back yet? Of course, you could never predict exactly where the big animals would be found. Besides, the snow was unusually deep this year, so perhaps that slowed their travel. But Konwatieni couldn't help worrying about Gannenstenhawi. She was still quite young; just seven winters had passed since she had come to Kahnawàke. And taking part in the annual hunt was new to her.

Then one afternoon, as warm sunshine melted the few remaining snowdrifts, the hunters' group appeared in the distance, walking slowly under their heavy burdens but waving with joy at the villagers who ran out to meet them. They passed through the gate and dropped their packs beside the village well. Others would take out the slabs of dried meat, and prepare them for storage in underground pits for safekeeping. It would be needed in the coming months, until there were new crops to harvest from the fields. Spring was always the leanest time of the whole year when it came to food. Everyone understood that and tried to eat just enough to get by.

Gannenstenhawi was very glad to be home. For the first day or two she stayed around the longhouse, just chatting with Konwatieni and Onwari about her adventures on the hunt. She described the happy surprise of meeting Arosen and his parents on the path coming home. But when she told them about falling in the river and how Arosen had saved her, it made her feel scared all over again. She recounted her dream about following a moose through the forest, and what wise old Tewennatetha had said about it. Konwatieni listened carefully and nodded. She guessed the dream's meaning, but decided not to say anything just yet.

The next Sunday Konwatieni went to the church for mass, and took Gannenstenhawi along. The priests said many prayers and gave thanks to God for the success of the hunt. They even mentioned Gannenstenhawi's rescue from the river. Arosen had saved her, they said, but without God's help he couldn't have done it. God watches over everything; nothing happens without His permission. Once more,

Gannenstenhawi relived the scary moment. She bowed her head and, in a whisper no one else could hear, gave her own prayer of thanks.

Sitting just a few seats away were Arosen and his father and mother. That day, after mass had ended, the priests were going to baptize Arosen. Gannenstenhawi stayed to watch, remembering her own baptism several years before. It was different this time, though. She had been a child, Arosen was a grown man. First, the priests asked him several questions: Did he truly believe in God? Did he know the Catholic prayers? Had he completely given up the longhouse religion? Arosen answered in a strong voice that yes, he loved God and only God, and yes, he had learned the prayers; besides, his parents were already Catholic. The priests seemed satisfied and went ahead with the ceremony. They sprinkled holy water on Arosen's head, recited some special prayers, and said he was a Catholic from then on.

Arosen and his parents moved into a house that was left empty when another family went back to the homeland. It was just a few doors away from Konwatieni's. As the days passed, he and Gannenstenhawi would run into each other while going to and from the fields, the church, the well. Sometimes they would stop to chat or laugh together. There was one afternoon when they found themselves in the same patch of forest across the river. Gannenstenhawi was grubbing for roots to add to Konwatieni's cook-pot, while Arosen was chopping down trees for firewood. They talked for hours and didn't do much work. When Gannenstenhawi got back, Konwatieni teased her about her feelings for Arosen. She blushed and looked down, but said nothing. Arosen thought he had never met such a pleasing young woman. Soon everyone in both families understood that they loved each other and wished to marry.

But first, there were certain Mohawk customs they had to follow. On a fine spring morning, Arosen and his mother and father put on their best clothing—buckskin tunics and feathered headdresses—and walked together to Konwatieni's house. Their visit had been planned ahead of time, so Gannenstenhawi and many of her relatives were waiting at the door when they arrived. After a brief greeting, everyone went inside. Konwatieni and Atonnion sat on a high bench at one end of the cabin, with Gannenstenhawi standing behind them. Arosen and his parents were directly opposite.

After a minute of silence, Konwatieni spoke in a solemn voice. "For what reason," she asked, "have you honored us with your presence today?"

It was Arosen's mother who replied (for in such matters, women always took charge). "We have come to propose that our brave son, Arosen, and your gracious daughter, Gannenstenhawi, be joined in the relation of marriage."

Konwatieni smiled slightly and sat up very straight. "We thank you," she said. "We will consult together and consider carefully what you suggest."

After two days of discussion among many of the relatives, Konwatieni led a return visit to Arosen's family longhouse and gave their response. "With gladness and respect," she announced, "we agree to your proposal. From this day forward, let our daughter and your son be as two eagles flying side by side across the endless sky."

Then, with the young couple standing shyly in the center, each family offered gifts to the other—strings of wampum, woven baskets, blankets, beaded jewelry. When that was over, Gannenstenhawi brought out a large pot of corn soup she had prepared especially for the occasion. Arosen took the first spoonful; then everyone else followed. And that was the final part of a Mohawk wedding.

But there was more to consider. Since Gannenstenhawi and Arosen were baptized Catholics, they also had to have a church wedding. So when another week had passed, they went to the large brick house next to the church, where the priests lived. They knocked on the front door and were shown in by a priest called Father Cholonec. The room they entered was unlike any they had seen before; it was called the great hall. The ceiling was very high, there were windows made of colored glass, and tall wooden armchairs stood against every wall. Gannenstenhawi felt uncomfortable right away and wondered if they should have come. Arosen, too, was doubtful.

But the priest seemed friendly and tried to put them at ease. "My dear children," he began, "you know you are always welcome here. Have you come perhaps to pray with us for your souls?"

Gannenstenhawi stared at the floor, leaving Arosen to respond, "No, Father, we say our prayers every night in our houses; we have another purpose today."

"Well and good," replied the priest with a gentle smile. "Please tell me what it is. I will be glad to help in any way I can."

"Thank you, Father," said Arosen. "I and this woman, whom I love with all my heart, wish to be married in the Catholic way; that is why we are here."

Gannenstenhawi looked up and saw a little shadow cross the priest's face; he seemed displeased. After a minute of thought, he gave his reply: "It would be difficult. Let me talk with my brothers." (He meant the other priests.) "You may come again tomorrow to hear our decision."

But when they arrived the next day and waited at the door, no one answered. And the next day, and the day after that, the same thing happened. Obviously, the priests wanted nothing to do with marrying them.

Gannenstenhawi could not imagine why. But the priests knew what she had put out of her mind so long ago: her birth and early years as an English child; her capture; her father, a famous Puritan minister who wished very much to get her back; the way many people in Massachusetts were upset by her having stayed with the Mohawks. When the priests considered her whole story, they thought that if she married an Indian, her father—and all the English—would get even more upset.

Finally, a message came from the church: Father Cholonec would see them after all. When they arrived, he was waiting in the same great hall. He sat stiffly in the tallest of the armchairs and motioned them to a bench below. He went right to the point. "My children," he said, "we have considered your request to be married in the church. It is impossible; we cannot grant it." He gave no reason, but instead looked away and began a prayer. At this Arosen stood up to speak. His voice was firm. "Father," he said, "we do not wish to do wrong. But we will never leave each other, no matter what you tell us. Our love unites us; we need nothing more from the church." Gannenstenhawi nodded her agreement, and the two of them prepared to leave.

The priest turned back in their direction. "In that case," he said, in a sharp tone, "you would live in sin, and God would condemn you, and your souls would be damned forever. Wait here while I speak again with my brothers." He left them standing near the door and went to another part of the residence. He returned a few minutes later. This time he brought a different message. "You give us no choice," he began. "We cannot let you defy the Lord by staying together without his blessing. Come again on Saturday at noontime and you shall have your wish."

And so they did. Konwatieni came with them. The big church seemed empty; no one else was there. The priests shortened the ceremony because they wanted it to be over as quickly and quietly as possible. There were a few prayers, but nothing more. Then Father Cholonec touched them both on the forehead and said the words that mattered most: "I pronounce you man and wife." They had the Lord's blessing after all.

CHAPTER FIFTEEN

A FINAL ANSWER

IF THE PRIESTS HAD HOPED TO KEEP THE
marriage secret, they soon were disappointed. The news
went quickly around the village and no one tried to stop
it. As the summer moved along, travelers carried it south
to the homeland, and from there it passed to the English
in Massachusetts. In Deerfield, John Williams heard it from
a neighbor who had been to Albany and met with several
Kahnawàke fur traders there. It left him sunk in despair.

As long as Eunice (to him, that remained her name) was
still young, he held out hope for her return. Eventually, he
believed, she would come to her senses and know where she
truly belonged. At that point, the Indians would realize how
wrong it was to keep her any longer against her (and his) will.
Other captives were coming home, by one means or another.

Three boys, Martin Kellogg, Thomas Baker, and Joseph Petty, had fled the village late one night and found their way back to Deerfield. The Indians had released several more in exchange for payment. Surely Eunice's turn would come.

But other factors weighed heavily against it. First was her having forgotten the English language. Second, her conversion to Catholicism. And now, worst of all, her marriage to a Kahnawàke man. Pledging herself and her life to an Indian! A savage! How could she? Reverend Williams found it shocking, impossible to understand. And he knew it would make the task of bringing her home even harder.

Still, he would never give up trying. He sent letters to Joseph Dudley, the Massachusetts governor, who promised to help. He wrote to the governor of Canada, Pierre de Rigaud de Vaudreuil, who seemed sympathetic but would not tell the Mohawks what to do. He urged merchants with business in Montreal to inquire about Eunice. He thought of going there himself, but the journey was long and difficult, and his duties as Deerfield's minister kept him very busy. Besides, he had a new family now, including three small children with his second wife. At last, in the summer of 1713, he saw a good chance to reach out to her. A merchant from Albany, John Schuyler, came to Deerfield for a visit. Schuyler was well-known among the Mohawks as a trading partner and friend. He had been to Kahnawàke before and would be going again soon. He promised John Williams that he would find Eunice and talk with her directly. He would do his very best to persuade her to come back to Massachusetts.

After a brief stop at his home in Albany, Schuyler began his journey, following the usual route through the wilderness up to Montreal. He had a pleasant meeting with Governor Vaudreuil, who lent him a horse to ride to Kahnawàke and appointed two men to act as his interpreters. Most people in the village, including Gannenstenhawi, could speak only the Mohawk language. Schuyler spoke English and Dutch, so translation would be necessary.

When Schuyler reached the village, he was met by three of the priests. They took him to the great hall, showed him to a couch where he might rest, offered him tea and biscuits, and began a discussion. Father Cholonec spoke for the rest. "We are glad to see you and hope to make you comfortable. May the Lord bless you and keep you always. Now, pray tell us why you have come today, that we might assist you."

Schuyler replied, "I thank you most heartily for your welcome, Father. My purpose is to speak with Eunice Williams, a lovely child cruelly taken from her family in Massachusetts by Mohawk warriors long ago and kept in this village ever since. Her father, Reverend John Williams—a man of great importance, a minister to the good people of the town called Deerfield—has sent me to bring her home at last."

"I believe," said Cholonec, "you refer to Marguerite, for that is the name with which we baptized her. It is many years since she came here. She is no longer a child. She was raised by a kind man, now gone to heaven, and his pious wife, with whom she still resides. She has her own husband now. She is much loved by the people of the village and is happy with her life here. I do not know that she would wish to leave."

At the mention of the husband, Schuyler's face darkened. "It was," he said, "very wrong of you to marry her. Her English blood cries out against it. That she should wed an Indian: how terrible . . ." His voice trailed off without finishing the sentence.

Cholonec spoke again. "At first we thought of this as you do now. We tried to stop them. We told them to wait; we avoided them as much as we could. But they insisted—refused our advice, kept coming and coming to press their wish upon us. At last they said they would stay together whether married or not. And so we decided it was better done in a church way than any other."

Schuyler stood up and spread his hands in dismay. "Then I must see her for myself. May it please you to inform her of my presence here." Cholonec sighed and told one of the younger priests to find Marguerite in her house and bring her to the residence.

While all this was happening, news of the merchant's arrival spread quickly through the village. His purpose was understood—it was nothing new, this idea of taking Gannenstenhawi away. When the priest arrived at her house, a crowd had gathered in front of the door, barring his entry.

Inside, Gannenstenhawi crouched in a corner with Arosen by her side. She was weeping. She told the others that she would not speak with the merchant. He was foolish, he did not know her at all. He did not see that this was her home, that she belonged here, nowhere else. She was a Mohawk, not an Englishwoman. She would not go to Massachusetts, not now, not ever.

Presently, Konwatieni came over, rested a hand on her shoulder, and spoke in a gentle tone. "My dear child, do not fear. You belong to our people. Nothing can take you from us. But this merchant has traveled far to see you. He has trade with our village; we must not displease him. Come, then, to the priests' residence. Your husband will stay beside you, and so will I."

Gannenstenhawi dared not refuse any longer. Reluctantly, she stood up, pulled a large blanket tight around her chest, and made her way to the door. Konwatieni took her arm; Arosen followed close behind. The men outside stepped back to let them pass. They walked slowly along the path that led to the residence. Father Cholonec was standing at the door as they came up.

"Dear Marguerite," he began. "We have been waiting for

you with the merchant from Albany, Mr. Schuyler. He is a good man and a friend to the village; his trade helps the people here. He has a message from your English father. Let us hear what he has to say." Gannenstenhawi looked down and said nothing. Her English father? By now she understood that he was the one who had sent the merchant to take her away.

She and the others went into the great hall. There were at least a dozen people there, priests and some of her Mohawk friends. Schuyler rose to greet her. At his bidding she sat in a chair, but with her head turned away from him.

"My dear Eunice," he said in a loud voice, "I am very pleased to meet with you." Of course, he did not speak in her language, so one of the interpreters had to translate.

But she caught the name Eunice and wondered, *What is this "Eunice"?* Her thoughts spun wildly. The name—she knew it somehow—began to open her memory. Pictures of things long forgotten came rushing into her mind. She saw herself in a room somewhere far away, in bed, fast asleep. But, all of a sudden, terrifying sounds—crashing, shouting, screaming—awakened her. She ran in the dark to hide . . . Another picture: She was walking on a snowy path in deep woods beside a frozen river. A hand reached down to steady her—a mother's hand. Then the hand was gone, the mother was gone . . . And another: She was in the village—this village—scared and anxious to leave. A man came to help her, but he couldn't. He tried, he failed. He had failed before. She stood at the gate, watching him go.

Gannenstenhawi had closed her eyes during these flashbacks. And when she opened them again, the merchant was going on with his talk. The interpreter translated, "I have come at the request of your father, Reverend John Williams. He has grieved for many years over your absence. He longs for your return. He prays every day for your soul. He honors the memory of your late mother, slain by savage enemies when you were still young. Since her death he has taken in holy wedlock a gracious and God-fearing gentlewoman; she is your stepmother now. She has borne him a son and two daughters. Your older brothers, Samuel and Stephen, are at college. Your youngest brother, Warham, is a fine Christian boy. The whole family awaits your return! Come back with me, child, come back to your home."

Everyone turned toward Gannenstenhawi. She looked uncomfortable. Her mind was bringing back more memories. The mother's hand taken from her on the trail—suddenly she understood. The man who had failed to protect her in several times of need also had failed to save the mother. Her English father? Of course! He was the one! And then to hear that he had gone and taken another wife! How wrong! How cruel! She couldn't forgive that. Her thoughts raced along at top speed, but her lips remained tightly closed.

Schuyler continued, his words more pleading, more urgent, than before. "The war is over; many of those who were taken from us are happily returned. You *must* come home. It is your duty to your father, to all who pray for you, to almighty God Himself. God puts each of us in a place of His choosing. He put you in Deerfield, with English parents and neighbors. It is not for us to question His ways."

Again, she made no reply.

Schuyler tried a new approach. Perhaps she would agree to a visit—a stay of a few days or weeks with her father, to see how it felt. In that case, he promised, "upon my word and honor, you shall have full liberty to return to this village if you wish."

Still, she was silent.

Schuyler paused, uncertain what else he could say. Then Father Cholonec stepped forward. "Dear child," he began. "What the merchant says is fair. You have lived a good while among us; we have cared for you and prayed with you as you rose into womanhood. But you are of a different blood from our Mohawk villagers. Go, then, with this good man. Meet with your father and others of your English family. You will decide then whether or not to remain with them. If you prefer the life here, you may return; you will always be welcome among us."

The two of them, the merchant and the priest, kept on at her for more than an hour. They repeated their arguments again and again; their voices became loud and strained. But still she sat there, unmoved. Finally, Cholonec insisted that she say something—anything—in reply. And so she did. She looked up and spoke, in a soft but distinct voice, two Mohawk words, *jaghte oghte*, which the interpreter translated as "maybe not." She was being polite; there was no "maybe" about it. What she meant was, "No! I won't go, not to stay, and not for a visit, either."

Schuyler was furious. "You should be ashamed!" he shouted in frustration. "If I had made the same fair proposal to the worst of Indians, I would have received a better answer."

At this, Arosen moved toward him to say a little more on her behalf. "Mr. Schuyler, it is plain. She is unwilling to leave us. She knows of the man you call her English father. She would gladly have gone to see him, had he not married again."

That is all he would say, and all Schuyler would ever learn about her reasons. It explained nothing. Of course her father had married again. He'd needed a wife, a helper, to start a new home; surely God approved of it.

There was nothing more to be done. Gannenstenhawi shifted uneasily in her chair. Her face was a mask, hiding her feelings underneath. Suddenly Schuyler stepped forward and grasped both of her hands in his. Alarmed, she pulled away. Then, flinging up his arms in disgust, he strode away from the residence.

After he got back to Albany, Schuyler wrote out a careful account of his meeting with Eunice. He sent a copy to John Williams in Deerfield. Of course, the entire Williams family was dismayed—crushed even—by what it said.

But this was her final answer: *jaghte oghte.* Maybe not. I won't go. I have a different life now. And I mean to keep it that way.

THE YEAR AFTER SCHUYLER WENT TO Kahnawàke, John Williams himself had a chance to visit. He was part of a group sent to Canada by the Massachusetts governor, Joseph Dudley, to discuss the return of all the captives still living there. He was told as soon as he reached Montreal that his daughter preferred not to see him. It would be pointless and distressing, she thought; why didn't he understand that? But he insisted, and finally he was allowed into the village. The two of them met in the priests' residence, but for only a few minutes. Her answer hadn't changed. He left in the same sorrowful state as when he had been there long before, soon after her capture. Only this time, she wasn't at the gate watching him go. She was a grown woman now, not a frightened child. And most important of all, she was a true Mohawk.

Decades of adult life lay ahead of her. She remained in Kahnawàke and raised a family. Together with Arosen, she had eight children, only two of whom, both daughters, survived to adulthood. The others died either in wars or from the diseases that swept again and again through the village. Both daughters grew up and married important Mohawk men.

From time to time, the Williamses in Deerfield would receive news of her. Usually it was very brief—she and her husband were "in health," or had passed through Albany while traveling south for trade—not much more. Her father prayed for her every day, sometimes publicly in church with his entire congregation. Then, in 1729, he took sick and died; there was a large funeral, at which his daughter's captivity and life in Canada were remembered with sorrow.

Surprisingly, though, reports came soon afterward that Eunice (always the family's name for her) was considering a visit to Massachusetts. Her brothers grew hopeful. Nothing happened for quite a few more years. But then, in the summer of 1740, it became definite. She and Arosen would be traveling to Albany and were ready to meet there with members of the Williams family. Two of her brothers, Stephen and Samuel, set out at once and found her waiting. They had what Stephen described as a "joyful, sorrowful" reunion; he meant that he was both very glad to see her and sad that their separation had lasted so long. From Albany they traveled to Longmeadow, Massachusetts, where Stephen was now the minister. The whole town turned out in welcome; in fact, people came from all over the colony (and from Connecticut) to see her. Everyone was curious about this person whose life had started out like theirs, yet was now so completely different. And maybe, they thought, she had finally decided to come home for good.

Eunice and Arosen were invited to stay as guests in Stephen's house, but chose instead to put up a little tent in the yard. The women of Longmeadow brought English dresses for her to wear, but she preferred her Indian blankets; she would stick with Mohawk custom. There was also the problem of communicating—whenever they wanted to converse, interpreters had to translate between English and Mohawk.

The town gave a dinner in her honor and held a special service in the church. Stephen and the other Williamses encouraged her—in fact, they begged her—to stay. But she said no, she wanted only to get to know her long-lost relatives, and also to claim a share of her father's estate. His will had included gifts to her of land and money. But this applied only if she were willing to resettle in Massachusetts, which was never her plan. So, after two very emotional weeks, she and Arosen left Longmeadow and returned to Canada. By now there was warmth on both sides; she seemed, as Stephen wrote in his diary, "very much affected" by the visit.

She promised to come back the next summer, and she did. This time she and Arosen traveled across Massachusetts and Connecticut, visiting different Williams relatives along the way. They stopped in Deerfield to see where she had been born. She was received by the governor in Boston, and he, too, tried his best to persuade her to stay. People everywhere were upset about her being an Indian; how much better it would be for her to become English again! At least that's what they thought; but of course, she didn't.

Two summers later she came for a third time, accompanied by several others in her Mohawk family. Again, she was warmly received. And again, there were high hopes for her permanent return. But it was not to be; visiting was still her aim, nothing more. When they pressed her about this, she tried to make them understand. She loved her Williams relatives in Massachusetts and was very glad to see them. But her home would always be Kahnawàke—and the Mohawks would remain her people.

There would be a gap of almost two decades before her fourth, and final, visit. That was a time of renewed war between the English and French colonies, and there was little chance for contact. But in 1761, when peace was at last restored, she and Arosen were able to visit Stephen once more. By now, all three of them were quite old, and they knew it was probably their last chance to see each other. As the visit came to an end, they embraced, wept, and spoke of their hope to be together someday in heaven.

Still, they remained in touch. In 1765 Stephen received news that Arosen had died and sent a letter of condolence. In the years that followed, more letters would pass between them. Of course, on her side someone had to translate and write in English for her. Her letters were signed "your faithful sister, Eunice Williams." This showed how much she felt reconnected with her Massachusetts relatives; with them at least, she was willing to be known by her English name.

In 1782 Stephen took ill and died just before his ninetieth birthday. But his sister lived on for another three years. By then she was the last survivor among all those captured in the Deerfield raid so long before.

Eunice's own death was noted in a book of records kept by the priests and preserved at the church ever since. Translated from French, one page read: "On the 26th of November 1785 we buried Marguerite, mother-in-law of Annasetegen. She was ninety-five years old." To the priests, she was still known as Marguerite. Annasetegen was the village chief. The record exaggerated her age; actually she was eighty-nine.

But her story does not end there. In years to come, her grandson, a fur trader and army scout, would sometimes visit his Williams relatives when passing through Massachusetts. Two of her great-grandsons were sent to Deerfield for schooling. Fifty years after her death, a large group of Mohawks went and stayed there a full week. Their purpose, they said, was to "visit the graves of our ancestors." Descendants of hers live in Kahnawàke today.

From Eunice, to A'ongote, to Marguerite, to Gannenstenhawi: Her different names are like headlines over her long and extraordinary life. And we who look back from more than two centuries later on, may still wonder at its meaning.

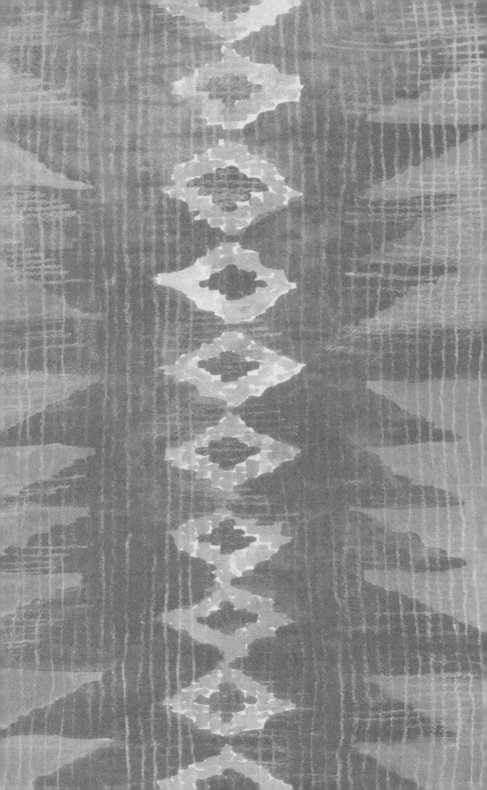

ALTHOUGH IT WAS WELL-KNOWN IN ITS own time, the story of Eunice Williams was gradually forgotten as the centuries passed. I first heard about it, some thirty years ago, from a graduate student who was writing a dissertation on the hundreds of captives taken from early New England. I was fascinated and wanted right away to know more.

I began research that would last almost a decade and take me to dozens of different archival sites. Deerfield, Longmeadow, and Boston in Massachusetts; Kahnawàke, Montreal, Quebec City, and Ottawa in Canada; and Paris, France, were the most important.

Gradually, I stitched together the central parts of the story. As with all historical research, there were both triumphs and disappointments. I felt fortunate in how much could be learned about the Mohawks of Kahnawàke, Eunice's home for more than eighty years. (The correct pronunciation is Gah-na-WAH-gee, with the accent on the third syllable.) But I was disappointed that many personal details of her life remained out of view. Once she was absorbed into the Mohawk community, she was destined to live as an ordinary woman. And like most ordinary women of that period—whether English, French, or Indian—her individual doings went largely unrecorded.

Eventually I reached the point of writing a book. Published in 1994, *The Unredeemed Captive: A Family Story from Early America* was aimed squarely at adult readers. When some of those suggested I write a children's version, I was intrigued. The idea stayed with me until, finally, I decided to act upon it.

This book is the result. It differs from the previous one in important ways. First, it concentrates on Eunice's childhood and early teenage years, the period when she was born and nurtured in a New England household, captured in the famous Deerfield raid of 1704, and then transplanted into what became her Mohawk family and community. Her adult life is briefly summarized, but not more than that, in the Epilogue. Second, the book offers details of her experience that go beyond the surviving evidence. Since much is known about her surroundings, the events included here *could* have happened to a girl like Eunice, although in many cases there is no proof that they actually did. For example, we have solid information about John Schuyler's visit in 1713, but her participation in a winter hunt is based on general information about the Mohawks. Similarly, the beliefs recounted for her benefit by a village elder conform closely with long-standing Mohawk tradition, but the occasion of their recounting is invented.

To say it differently: While the frame of the story is historically real—Eunice Williams was a *real* person, who *really was* captured by Indians, and *really did* refuse to return to her original home—much of her life has had to be imagined, based on research about that period and educated guesswork. Thus it seems best to identify the book as historical fiction.

Still, that need not count against it. We can never know the absolute truth about lives in the past. All history is, in one way or another, the product of our imagination.

Chapter One: Wintertime

page 5: "You are a smart child . . ." On schools and schooling in early New England, see James Axtell, *The School Upon a Hill: Education and Society in Colonial New England* (W. W. Norton, New York, 1976).

pages 6–7: tried to distract herself by humming tunes . . . On children's lives in early New England, see Alice Morse Earle, *Child Life in Colonial Days* (Macmillan, New York, 1899); John Demos, *A Little Commonwealth: Family Life in Plymouth Colony* (Oxford University Press, New York, 1970), chapter 4; Edmund S. Morgan, *The Puritan Family: Religion and Domestic Relations in Seventeenth-Century New England* (Harper & Row, New York, 1966), chapter 2.

page 7: He also preached sermons . . . There are many studies of early New England religious life. See, for example, Charles Hambrick-Stowe, *The Practice of Piety: Puritan Devotional Disciplines in Seventeenth-Century New England* (University of North Carolina Press, Chapel Hill, NC, 1986).

Chapter Two: A Baby Sister

page 10: what they called swaddling . . . On childbirth in colonial New England, see Richard W. Wertz and Dorothy C. Wertz, *Lying-In: A History of Childbirth in America* (Yale University Press, New Haven, CT, 1989), chapter 1.

Chapter Three: Enemy Attack

page 15: the moon shone red . . . On Deerfield's preparations for war, see George Sheldon, *A History of Deerfield, Massachusetts* (E. A. Hall & Co., Greenfield, MA, 1895), volume 1, chapter 11. A more recent, definitive history of Deerfield is Richard I. Melvoin, *New England Outpost: War and Society in Colonial Deerfield* (W. W. Norton, New York, 1989).

page 17: But it was too late . . . For details of the Deerfield raid, see John Demos, *The Unredeemed Captive: A Family Story from Early America* (Alfred A. Knopf, New York, 1994), chapter 1. For a firsthand account, see John Williams, *The Redeemed Captive Returning to Zion* (Forgotten Books,

Boston, MA, 1774), pp. 44–47. Original documents about the raid are reprinted in Sheldon, *A History of Deerfield, Massachusetts*, volume 1, chapter 11; see especially pp. 302–03.

Chapter Four: The Journey

page 20: with every footstep . . . The journey to Canada is described in Demos, *The Unredeemed Captive*, pp. 25–35. See also Williams, *The Redeemed Captive*, pp. 47–64. Some years ago a plaque was installed at the site of Mrs. Williams's death alongside the Green River just to the north of Deerfield.

page 23: Eunice cried herself to sleep. Ibid., pp. 48–49.

page 23: she, like Warham, was carried. Ibid., pp. 54, 65.

Chapter Five: Canada

page 28: its people were called the Kahnawakenerons. On the history of Kahnawàke, see Demos, *The Unredeemed Captive*, chapter 6, and Edward J. Devine, *Historic Caughnawaga* (Messenger Press, Montreal, 1922), passim.

page 28: that surrounded the village. On the layout of the village, see Joseph François Lafitau, *Customs of the American Indians Compared with the Customs of Primitive Times*, two volumes (originally published in Paris, France, 1724;

reprinted by the Champlain Society, Toronto, Canada, 1974), volume 2, pp. 16–19.

page 28: Arakwente gave a shout . . . For a description of housing in Kahnawàke, see ibid., volume 2, p. 19.

page 30: metal pots and barrels . . . On domestic life among the Kahnawàke Mohawks, see Demos, *The Unredeemed Captive*, chapter 7. For firsthand description of many details, see Lafitau, *Customs of the American Indians*, passim.

Chapter Six: The Rest of the Family

page 38: Her gravestone was carefully engraved . . . On events immediately following the Deerfield raid, see Demos, *The Unredeemed Captive*, chapter 2, and Sheldon, *A History of Deerfield, Massachusetts*, chapter 11. The gravestone of Mrs. Eunice Williams, mother of the captive girl of the same name, stands near the center of the old burial ground in Deerfield.

page 39: Only much later . . . The old Mohawk words included here are taken from a list made by the anonymous author of *A Narrative of a Journey into the Mohawk and Oneida Country*, 1634–35, reprinted in *Narratives of New Netherland*, J. Franklin Jameson, ed. (Charles Scribner's Sons, New York, 1909), pp. 157–62.

page 39: French boys who lived nearby. On the placement of the Williams children following their arrival in Canada, see Demos, *The Unredeemed Captive*, p. 35. Details of their experiences are imagined.

Chapter Seven: The Visit

page 42: he was very eager to get there. For John Williams's own account of this event, see his *Redeemed Captive*, pp. 66–67.

Chapter Eight: Left Behind

page 46: They prayed also for his children . . . On the general topic of Indian captivity, see June Namias, *White Captives: Gender and Ethnicity on the American Frontier* (University of North Carolina Press, Chapel Hill, NC, 1993). Older but still useful studies are C. Alice Baker, *True Stories of New England Captives*, (Cambridge, MA, 1897), and Emma Lewis Coleman, *New England Captives Carried to Canada*, two volumes (Southworth Press, Portland, ME, 1925).

page 47: Reverend Williams for Captain Baptiste. Demos, *The Unredeemed Captive*, pp. 16–17.

page 49: the townspeople looked on and cheered. On John Williams's return, and his sermon in particular, see ibid., pp. 49–50, 60–65.

page 51: she was an Indian girl now. Ibid., p. 146.

Chapter Nine: Becoming a Different Person

page 53: instead of actual corn. The details of farming as practiced in Kahnawàke are scattered throughout Lafitau, *Customs of the American Indians*; see especially volume 2, pp. 54–55, 60–64, 105, 288, 290–91. For a quick summary, see Demos, *The Unredeemed Captive*, pp. 160–61.

page 54: it was time to stop. Such dances among the Mohawks are described in Lafitau, *Customs of the American Indians*, volume 1, pp. 323–24.

page 54: Corn was their most important food . . . On eat-all feasts, see ibid., volume 2, p. 61. On the foods typically consumed, ibid., volume 2, pp. 62–68.

page 55: if you dropped it or let it fall . . . This girls' game is described in ibid., volume 2, p. 199.

page 55: or even a spanking. Ibid., volume 1, p. 361.

page 56: it took about a year . . . Demos, *The Unredeemed Captive*, pp. 141–42. For details of Mohawk naming and renaming practices, see the works cited in endnotes 3–6 in ibid., pp. 282–83.

page 57: As the family arrived . . . On the role of certain village elders—shamans, we call them now—see Lafitau,

Customs of the American Indians, volume 1, pp. 237–38, and volume 2, p. 210.

page 58: These same clans were in every Mohawk village . . . On Mohawk clans, see ibid., volume 1, pp. 287–88. See also Demos, *The Unredeemed Captive*, p. 163.

page 59: called by different names. On beliefs about Shonkwaiiatihson, see Lafitau, *Customs of the American Indians*, volume 1, p. 102.

page 62: her original name, Eunice. Ibid., pp. 151–52. On the history of the Catholic Church in Kahnawàke, see Devine, *Historic Caughnawaga*.

Chapter Ten: Learning Their Beliefs

page 64: a hole in a tree in the forest. Lafitau discusses wampum and its various uses in *Customs of the American Indians*, volume 1, pp. 308–10.

page 66: *How will I recognize him?* There are multiple sources for this story of Iroquois origins, and versions differ. For an excellent summary of these, see Christopher Vecsey, "The Story and Structure of the Iroquois Confederacy," in *Journal of the American Academy of Religion, LIV* (1986), 79–106. See also Daniel K. Richter, *Ordeal of the Longhouse: The People of the Iroquois League in the Era of the European Colonization* (University of North Carolina Press, Chapel Hill, NC, 1992), chapter 1, and

Douglas M. George-Kanentiio and Joanne Shenandoah-Tekalihwa: *Skywoman: Legend of the Iroquois* (Clear Light Publishers, Santa Fe, NM, 1998).

page 67: *when I grow up.* Again, there are multiple sources and versions. See Darren Bonaparte, *Creation and Confederation: The Living History of the Iroquois*, (Wampum Chronicles, New York, 2008), chapter 6. For a contemporary account, see Lafitau, *Customs of the American Indians*, volume 1, p. 86.

page 69: how lucky the nations were . . . For a full discussion of this legend, see Matthew Dennis, *Cultivating a Landscape of Peace: Iroquois-European Encounters in Seventeenth-Century America*, (Cornell University Press, Ithaca, NY, 1995), chapter 3.

page 70: to act always in accord with them. On the power accorded to dreams by the Mohawks, see Richter, *The Ordeal of the Longhouse*, pp. 25–28, and, for a contemporary account, Lafitau, *Customs of the American Indians*, volume 1, pp. 231–35.

page 70: ". . . there is only joy." Mohawk beliefs about the soul and the afterlife are described in ibid., volume 1, pp. 253, 258.

Chapter Eleven: Tragedy Strikes
page 75: And she had no wish to leave. See Demos, *The Unredeemed Captive*, pp. 84–97.

page 76: If she remembered anything . . . Ibid., p. 165. See also Lafitau, *Customs of the American Indians*, volume 1, p. 69.

page 78: Kahnawàke had already suffered . . . On mortality among the Kahnawàke Mohawks, see Demos, *The Unredeemed Captive*, pp. 158–59.

page 79: help them fight the disease. Sweathouse treatment is described in Lafitau, *Customs of the American Indians*, volume 2, pp. 207–09.

page 80: Grieving his loss, Hiawata . . . On Kahnawàke funerary practices, see ibid., volume 2, pp. 218–30.

page 81: withdraw from mourning. On mourning practices, especially for women, see ibid., volume 2, pp. 242–43.

Chapter Twelve: Other Worlds

page 83: The village chiefs held long discussions . . . Demos, *The Unredeemed Captive*, p. 90. (See the works cited in endnotes 43–45, in ibid., p. 271, for original sources on these diplomatic maneuvers.)

page 84: deerskin tunic and hair decorated with pink flowers. Ibid., p. 155. On Mohawk naming practices, see Elisabeth Tooker, "Women in Iroquois Society," in

Extending the Rafters: Interdisciplinary Approaches to Iroquoian Studies (State University of New York Press, Albany, NY, 1984), Michael K. Foster, Jack Campasi, and Marianne Mithun, eds., p. 112.

page 85: Gannenstenhawi was exhausted. For a general account of the fur trade in this region, see Thomas Elliott Norton, *The Fur Trade in Colonial New York, 1686–1776*, (University of Wisconsin Press, Madison, WI, 1974). On participation by the Kahnawàke Mohawks in particular, see Jean Lunn, "The Illegal Fur Trade Out of New France, 1713–60," in *Report of the Annual Meeting of the Canadian Historical Association*, volume 18, number 1, 1939, pp. 61–76.

page 86: lacy bonnets on their heads. For a description of Albany in this period, see Demos, *The Unredeemed Captive*, pp. 188–89.

page 89: following a few paces behind. On slavery in colonial New York, see Edgar J. McManus, *A History of Negro Slavery in New York* (Syracuse University Press, Syracuse, NY, 1966).

page 89: jewelry as a mark of honor. For a contemporary account of Mohawk trade with Europeans, including the articles most often given and received, see Lafitau, *Customs of the American Indians*, volume 2, p. 184.

page 91: trade only with the French. On the laws against trading across national lines, see Lunn, "The Illegal Fur Trade Out of New France, 1713–60."

Chapter Thirteen: A Winter Hunt

page 94: the heavy burdens of the trip home. For details of the winter hunt, see Lafitau, *Customs of the American Indians*, volume 2, pp. 110–119.

Chapter Fourteen: A Marriage

page 105: they loved each other and wished to marry. On Kahnawàke customs on courtship and marriage, see Lafitau, *Customs of the American Indians*, volume 1, pp. 342–44. See also Demos, *The Unredeemed Captive*, p. 155.

page 109: They had the Lord's blessing after all. This portrayal of their attempts to be married in the church is based on the account sent by John Schuyler following his visit to Kahnawàke; see Demos, *The Unredeemed Captive*, pp. 104–05.

Chapter Fifteen: A Final Answer

page 111: Surely Eunice's turn would come. On the return of captives from Canada to Deerfield, see ibid., pp. 43–51.

page 112: so translation would be necessary. Schuyler's account of his visit to Kahnawàke is printed in full in Sheldon, *A History of Deerfield, Massachusetts*, volume 1, pp. 349–50.

page 118: "She would gladly have gone to see him . . ." Arosen's words about Gannenstenhawi's willingness to visit her father "had he not married again" are quoted in Schuyler's account of the visit; see ibid., p. 350.

Epilogue

page 121: she was a true Mohawk. See Demos, *The Unredeemed Captive*, pp. 113–16.

page 122: his daughter's captivity and life in Canada . . . Ibid., pp. 173–74.

page 123: come home for good. Ibid., chapter 9.

page 125: known by her English name. Ibid., pp. 231–32.

page 125: actually she was eighty-nine. Ibid., p. 237.

page 126: Descendants of hers live in Kahnawàke today. Ibid., pp. 246–52.

C. Alice Baker, *True Stories of New England Captives* (E. A. Hall & Co., Cambridge, MA, 1897). An early, charmingly written account of several captives' stories, including that of Eunice Williams.

Emma Lewis Coleman, *New England Captives Carried to Canada,* two volumes (Southworth Press, Portland, ME, 1925). A detailed compilation of hundreds of cases.

John Demos, *The Unredeemed Captive: A Family Story from Early America* (Alfred A. Knopf, New York, 1994). The book on which this one is based.

Edward J. Devine, *Historic Caughnawaga* (Messenger Press, Montreal, 1922). A detailed history of Kahnawake (note variant spelling), largely from the viewpoint of the Catholic Church.

Douglas M. George-Kanentiio and Joanne Shenandoah-Tekalihwa, *Skywoman: Legends of the Iroquois* (Clear Light Publishers, Santa Fe, NM, 1998).

Evan Haefeli and Kevin Sweeney, *Captive Histories: English, French, and Native Narratives of the 1704 Deerfield Raid* (University of Massachusetts Press, Amherst, MA, 2006). Several firsthand accounts of the 1704 raid.

————, *Captors and Captives: The 1704 French and Indian Raid on Deerfield* (University of Massachusetts Press, Amherst, MA, 2005). A detailed examination of the 1704 raid, with conclusions somewhat different from those presented here.

Joseph François Lafitau, *Customs of the American Indians Compared with the Customs of Primitive Times*, two volumes (originally published in Paris, France, 1724; reprinted by the Champlain Society, Toronto, Canada, 1974). William N. Fenton and Elizabeth L. Moore, eds. The indispensable primary source on Kahnawàke and its people during the time of Eunice Williams's residency. For several years, Lafitau was a priest at Kahnawàke.

Richard Melvoin, *New England Outpost: War and Society in Colonial Deerfield* (W. W. Norton, New York, 1989). The definitive modern history of Deerfield in the colonial era.

June Namias, *White Captives: Gender and Ethnicity on the American Frontier* (University of North Carolina Press, Chapel Hill, NC, 1993). An overview of Indian captivities from the colonial era through the nineteenth century.

Daniel Richter, *The Ordeal of the Longhouse: The People of the Iroquois League in the Era of European Colonization* (University of North Carolina Press, Chapel Hill, NC, 1992). A careful study of Iroquoian society and culture in the colonial era.

George Sheldon, *A History of Deerfield, Massachusetts,* two volumes (E. A. Hall & Co., Greenfield, MA, 1895). An early and exhaustive account of Deerfield history, including many primary sources presented verbatim.

ACKNOWLEDGMENTS

I am indebted to family members and friends, for valuable assistance as I went along with this project.

To Michael Demos, Jill Lepore, and Elise Broach, for their crucial response to the very first of its draft chapters.

To Violet Demos, Clover Demos, and Alison Demos, for reading the whole story while still in manuscript form and giving it an important thumbs-up.

To Virginia Demos, life partner and insightful critic of all my work, for important suggestions about character and plot.